Going Google

Going Google

Powerful **Tools** for 21st Century Learning

Jared Covili

CORWIN
A SAGE Company

CORWIN
A SAGE Company

FOR INFORMATION:

Corwin
A SAGE Company
2455 Teller Road
Thousand Oaks, California 91320
(800) 233-9936
www.corwin.com

SAGE Publications Ltd.
1 Oliver's Yard
55 City Road
London EC1Y 1SP
United Kingdom

SAGE Publications India Pvt. Ltd.
B 1/I 1 Mohan Cooperative Industrial Area
Mathura Road, New Delhi 110 044
India

SAGE Asia-Pacific Pte. Ltd.
3 Church Street
#10-04 Samsung Hub
Singapore 049483

Acquisitions Editor: Debra Stollenwerk
Associate Editor: Desirée A. Bartlett
Editorial Assistant: Kimberly Greenberg
Production Editor: Amy Schroller
Copy Editor: Teresa Herlinger
Typesetter: C&M Digitals (P) Ltd.
Proofreader: Charlotte J. Waisner
Indexer: Maria Sosnowski
Cover Designer: Bryan Fishman
Permissions Editor: Adele Hutchinson

All figure images are used with permission of Google Inc.,
unless noted otherwise.

Printed in the United States of America

Library of Congress Cataloging-in-Publication Data

Covili, Jared.

Going Google: powerful tools for 21st century learning / Jared
Covili.

pages cm
Includes bibliographical references and index.

ISBN 978-1-4129-9878-9 (pbk. : alk. paper)

1. Internet in education. 2. Google. I. Title.

LB1044.87.C685 2012
004.67'8071—dc23   2012003505

This book is printed on acid-free paper.

MIX
Paper from
responsible sources
FSC
www.fsc.org   FSC® C014174

14 15 16 10 9 8 7 6 5 4 3

Contents

Preface

As a technology trainer, I've developed a number of courses to help teachers utilize computers and the Internet. A few years ago, I looked to create a new class that tapped into an expressed need for modern educators: Where can teachers find high-quality, free tools that allow their students to achieve the skills outlined for 21st century learners? The answer came back in a word—Google.

In the past decade, Google has expanded its role from simply being the leader in online searching, to transforming the way in which we communicate with one another. In an era when teachers are being asked to provide more information with little to no financial resources, using Google's free resources may be the best solution to "leave no child behind." And yet, many teachers have a limited idea of the various tools included in the Google library. This book will explore the wide array of Google tools from a K–12 educator's perspective, not simply focusing on how to use the tools, but also answering the larger questions of why use these tools and how can my students accomplish 21st century learning goals if we utilize Google tools.

This book is broken down into three major areas. Each of these areas reflects a core objective from the Skills for 21st Century Learners. They are as follows: Communicating and Collaborating, Creativity and Innovation, and Critical Thinking and Problem Solving. As we explore these different pedagogical elements, you'll find that various Google tools are used to illustrate how teachers can reach these objectives.

As we discuss the various tenets of 21st century learning skills, I hope you'll find this book addresses three essential areas for K–12 teachers:

1. Which Google tools are essential for achieving 21st century learning skills?

2. How can these tools improve learning and help teachers in their everyday classroom activity?

3. What are some practical lesson plan activities teachers can use with different Google tools as part of their student-centered projects?

To help in digesting key points and features, for each of the main Google tools, you'll find the book has a highlight—Five Things to Know About—at the beginning of the chapter. Also, classroom activities and projects are separated with their own unique heading. This will make the step-by-step instructions easier to find and follow. At the end of most of the chapters, you'll find two other highlights for teachers—More Ideas for Going Google and Tips for Going Google. These are quick ideas meant to further your use of the tools and provide an additional framework for classroom application. You will also find a useful glossary at the end of the book. Glossary terms in the text are denoted by boldface italics. Buttons or menu items to select on your computer screen, such as **Save** or **Translate**, are denoted by boldface type.

Another important feature found throughout *Going Google* is the use of screen captures. These images are designed to help illustrate concepts and provide guidance for accomplishing activities. The screen captures are time sensitive, so their content won't be relevant forever, but they provide a valuable resource to help you and your students visualize different Google tools in action.

Going Google: Powerful Tools for 21st Century Learning should be seen as a handy reference to use with all the other tools in your digital teacher tool belt. I hope you'll learn some new things about the Google you thought you knew. Thanks for joining me in the journey.

Acknowledgments

Corwin would like to recognize the following individuals for taking the time to provide their editorial insight and guidance:

James Anderson
Principal
Canaseraga Central School District
Canaseraga, NY

Karen Canfield
Principal
Pioneer Intermediate School
Noble, OK

Avis Canty
Special Needs and Fast Forward Reading Lab Instructor
Tanglewood Middle School
Greenville, SC

A. L. Hough-Everage
Associate Professor of Education
Brandman University
Victorville, CA

Jane Hunn
Science Teacher
Tippecanoe Valley Middle School
Akron, IN

Joan Irwin
Professional Development
Newark, DE

Rose Cherie Reissman
Literacy Consultant/Teacher Educator
Mind Lab/New City Department of Education Literacy Consultant
New York, NY

Sara Stewart
Project Facilitator, Instructional Technology
Curriculum and Professional Development
Clark County School District
Las Vegas, NV

Rick Yee
Principal
McAuliffe School
Saratoga, CA

About the Author

 **Jared Covili** is a professional development trainer at the Utah Education Network (UEN) in Salt Lake City. Jared specializes in teaching strategies for classroom integration of technology such as webpage design, geospatial learning, web 2.0 tools, and digital devices. Jared received his bachelor's degree in English and his master's degree in Instructional Design and Educational Technology from the University of Utah. His background includes four years as a secondary Language Arts teacher. Besides his work at UEN, Jared is involved with the Utah Coalition for Educational Technology (UCET) and served as president of the organization for 2011–2012. Jared also works as an adjunct faculty member in the College of Education at the University of Utah, where he teaches technology integration classes to undergraduate students.

Thanks to Tara, Kennedy, Alex, and Dylan.

*Only you know how often I was an absentee
husband and father while working on this project.*

Introduction

I recently read a bumper sticker posted on a colleague's cubicle that stated "I've Gone Google." *What?* How can someone "go Google"? Sure, we all use Google's search engine on a daily basis, but beyond finding information for work and home, can someone truly "go Google"? I started asking myself, what is the impact that "going Google" can have for teachers and students in the classroom?

What was once a start-up company run out of the garage by a couple of Stanford grad students has become one of the biggest companies in the world. Google spent its first few years developing the number one search engine on the web. For many, that's the only thing they know about Google—it's a search engine. But Google is so much more.

Google has spent the past decade developing an entire suite of tools that have revolutionized the way in which we use the Internet. These tools have made the world a smaller place by giving users a chance to work virtually from anywhere, with anyone, at any time they choose. Google has taken advantage of its size and ability to create a large scope for making these tools available to teachers and students—for free.

> Google's mission is to organize the world's information and make it universally accessible and useful. With regard to education, our goal is to leverage Google's strengths and infrastructure to increase access to high-quality open educational content and technology, more specifically, in science, engineering, technology and math. We support access to computing curriculum and educational technology for all students, leveling the playing field so that students and educators alike have the opportunity to shape the technologies of their future. The creators of tomorrow's innovations are everywhere, ready to be engaged and inspired. (Google, n.d.-a, n.p.)

So, what does it mean to "go Google" in your classroom? In a nutshell, it means taking advantage of the educational applications, or "apps," created and shared by Google as part of your curriculum. Whether it's as basic as conducting a search for a research paper, or as complicated as using Google Earth to develop an interactive virtual tour, "going Google" implies that teachers and students utilize Google tools to help them achieve 21st century skills.

■ THE WORLD HAS CHANGED

Over the past 15 years, the world has changed for our students. The students of today have been exposed to more media than any previous generation. Just look at the numbers:

- 89 percent of 18- to 24-year-old Americans are online.
- Digital Natives aged 12 to 24 spend 4.5 hours a day viewing screen media (TV, Internet, Internet video, mobile video), excluding games.
- 82 percent of seventh- to twelfth-graders "media multitask" while doing homework, e.g., IM, TV, Web surfing, etc. (Frontline, 2010, n.p.)

The problem is, our classrooms haven't changed. Look inside classrooms across the United States and you'll find a similar arrangement to those of the past century. Students are lined up neatly in rows with the desks facing a board with text written on it. Sure, the board may be a white board instead of a chalkboard, but the method of delivering materials to students is far behind the way in which students absorb material from their portable devices and computers.

Jim Shelton (2011), Assistant Deputy Secretary for Innovation and Improvement in the U.S. Department of Education, describes the situation in American classrooms:

> For too many of our students around the country, "boring" has become the adjective of choice to describe their experiences in the classroom. Students have been locked down by the concept of seat time and locked out of the technological revolution that has transformed nearly every sector of American society, except for education" (n.p.).

■ TWENTY-FIRST CENTURY SKILLS AND THE MODERN CLASSROOM

As we've moved from a paper-and-pencil past toward a 21st century classroom, we know that the classroom needs to progress. Marc Prensky (2010), founder of Games2Learn, looked at the changes our education system needs to undergo. He says,

> The reason a lot of people are stuck, I think, is because they confuse the old ways, the best ways of doing something once, with the best ways of doing those things forever. So it's not that kids shouldn't learn to communicate. It's not that they shouldn't learn to express complex ideas. Of course they should still learn all those things. Those are what we call the verbs. The nouns that they use, whether it's the essay or the paper or the writing or whatever it is, or whether it's the video or the podcast or the- [sic] that's what changes. (n.p.)

We know that our education system needs to improve, but what skills are necessary to empower our students for the jobs of tomorrow? Let's look over the list of skills emphasized for 21st century classrooms, and you'll find that technology's influence is evidenced throughout.

Communication and Collaboration

Our classrooms should strive to reflect an environment in which students are comfortable sharing their ideas with one another and with external partners as well. The modern work environment demands that employees be able to communicate their thoughts. Simply working on worksheets or taking a bubble sheet test isn't going to be a huge benefit for students looking to participate in the 21st century.

> Students of today enter an increasingly globalized world in which technology plays a vital role. They must be good communicators, as well as great collaborators. The new work environment requires responsibility and self-management, as well as interpersonal and project-management skills that demand teamwork and leadership. (Pearlman, n.d., n.p.).

Collaborative projects were once seen as somewhat of a novelty, but now are essential for working in the Internet age. Technology has made work location relatively meaningless—students can work in collaborative groups from anywhere. Yet so many of our classes incorporate assignments in which students work independently, confined to desks and rarely involving their classmates. A 21st century classroom looks to engage learners in collaborative groups, where learning takes place in and out of school.

Creativity and Innovation

Most American classrooms can be described as rigid, traditional, even boring—this is not the environment where creativity and innovation typically flourish. Whether it's due to the amount of material that needs to be covered in order to prepare for a standardized test, or the traditional nature of teaching in the current classroom model, bringing in new ideas and allowing students to explore their own creativity is a tremendous challenge facing many classrooms.

Former North Carolina Governor Jim Hunt (2010) shared the following concerning the need for creative thinking in our schools:

> A creative mindset is in increasingly high demand: employers are vying for workers who are able to dream big and deliver big with the next must-have product. Creative thinking fuels innovation, it leads to new goods and services, creates jobs and delivers substantial economic rewards. However, without adequately cultivating creativity in our schools at the state and local level, states like my home state of North Carolina will not be able to compete with other states and countries who already do. (n.p.)

We need to use technology-related activities to facilitate creativity and promote innovation with our students. Kids are excited to show what they know, by creating projects that demonstrate their skills. For a 21st century classroom to be effective, our assignments need to give students more than random facts for an upcoming exam; they need to provide students with the opportunity to design projects that inspire and motivate them.

Critical Thinking and Problem Solving

For several years, there has been an assumption on the part of parents and teachers that our children aren't learning as much as they used to. Our national test scores have gone down over the past decade, and there is a growing sense that it is due to the overabundance of available technology.

A 2008 study reviewed test scores of 800 thirteen- and fourteen-year-olds and compared them with similar tests of teens from 1976, a generation ago. The results? In one test, only one in ten of the current teens tested with top scores, down from one in four twenty years ago. In another, only one in twenty reached the top score compared to one in five from the 1976 batch. (Jordan, 2008, n.p.)

Is technology really to blame for the decrease in test scores? Here is the challenge for the modern teacher—we need to capitalize on our students' interest in and ability to use different technologies, but we don't want to isolate the technologies to the point that computers do the thinking for our students. As Jason Levy (quoted in Dretzin, 2010), principal of I.S. 339 in New York, stated, "Kids are going to need to be fluent in technology. They're going to need to be excellent at communication. They're going to need to be problem solvers. That's just the way the world is now" (n.p.).

One thing we can agree on: New technologies are going to continue to impact the classroom. A teacher of 21st century learners is going to need to use these technologies to enhance their critical thinking and problem solving skills, not replace them.

■ HOW TO USE THIS BOOK

Going Google isn't like your typical *Technology for Idiots* textbook. Learning how to use the different tools in the Google library is part of the goal, but you should also come to understand how to use the tools as part of an effective teaching strategy. That being said, *Going Google* wasn't designed to be followed from cover to cover, either. Rather, you should be able to scan quickly to any given section of the book to learn more about a tool and its classroom application.

The book's goals include allowing readers to do the following:

- Preview five major points to consider about each tool or group of tools at the beginning of the chapter or section.
- Discover ideas for implementing a Google tool in your instruction.

- Explore how the tools help students to meet national standards. Chapters begin with a reference to one of the National Education Technology Standards (*NETS*) for either teachers (NETS-T) or students (NETS-S). You will also find references to the Framework for 21st Century Learning in various chapters, developed by the Partnership for 21st Century Skills.
- Observe timely screen shots to help you visualize what you're learning.
- Find tips for "going Google" at the end of most chapters.

Because some of the terms used in *Going Google* may be considered technology jargon or "geek speak," I've included a glossary at the end of the book to help you understand unfamiliar words or concepts (Glossary terms are denoted by boldface italics.). I've tried my best to explain terms like HTML and RSS, but some of these acronyms are tough to illustrate quickly. The glossary should help clear up any misconceptions or confusing terms.

It's important to note that the tool tutorials in this book can't stay current forever. Google prides itself on innovation, and the tools in its library are always changing in their look and feel. Just while writing this book, Gmail, Calendar, Blogger, Docs, Sites, Reader, iGoogle, Picasa, and Search all had changes in the way they look. I want you to learn the essential features found within each of the tools. You'll always be able to copy and paste in Google Docs, whether the shortcut is found in the edit menu or not. No book can account for the stylistic changes Google will make, but I hope this book will help you learn the tools' important features and how they can be incorporated into your curriculum

POWERFUL TOOLS FOR ■ 21ST CENTURY CLASSROOMS

The premise of this book is simple: Educators want to use the best tools to engage their students and prepare them for their future. Google has created a comprehensive library of tools that can help teachers accomplish the goal of developing 21st century learners. After reading this book, there are a few things I hope you'll want to do.

- Explore the skills that students will need, moving forward in the 21st century.
- Learn about the different Google tools and discover how you can leverage the various programs in your classroom.
- Identify several classroom projects you can incorporate into your curriculum.

If you've only used Google as a search engine, this book should provide you with an overview of a variety of tools you can use with your students. If you've been using Google tools for a long time, I hope you'll see some new ways in which you can incorporate the programs you love into your classroom curriculum. Who knows? Maybe by the end of our time together, you'll have "gone Google" as well.

Part I

Communicating and Collaborating

Over the past decade, the demands of the modern workforce have shifted. No longer is the factory model of production a viable solution for educating our students. Collaborating with colleagues has become the norm in the business world, and yet our classrooms are still stuck in a 19th century framework of desks lined up in neat little rows. For the past 150 years, students have been expected to work on projects independent of one another, even though they are sitting right next to each other. The question has to be asked: Why? With so many advances in technology and a deeper understanding of learning theory, why are we still doing things the same way they were done so long ago? Tradition. Google tools offer one method of breaking down the constraints of the traditional classroom by providing students with the ability to work on projects at any time, with anyone, in any place. This is an example of the kind of change our classroom needs. Teachers know it, students know it, and our leaders know it.

> Schools must be more than information factories; they must be incubators of exploration and invention. Educators must be more than information experts; they must be collaborators in learning, seeking new knowledge and constantly acquiring new skills alongside their students. Students must be fully engaged in school—intellectually, socially, and emotionally. This level of engagement requires the chance to work on interesting and relevant projects, the use of technology environments and resources, and access to an extended social network of adults and peers who are supportive and safe. (U.S. Department of Education, 2010, n.p.)

Collaboration involves much more than simply working together on a project with others. Collaborative activities ask students and teachers to engage with one another, learn from one another, and rely on one another as an integral part of their education.

> Collaborative projects really make for an excellent education experience not only because students bounce ideas off each other and improve each other's writing skills, but also because the process itself teaches them how to work well with others—a valuable skill for everyone. (Richard Ellwood, Technology Coordinator and Digital Arts Teacher, Columbia Secondary School, Google, n.d.-c)

■ CREATING A COLLABORATIVE CLASSROOM USING GOOGLE

We've seen how the classroom needs to be updated. In order for our students to stay competitive on a global scale, we need to help them develop the necessary skills. In the Framework for 21st Century Learning (Partnership for 21st Century Skills, 2004), collaboration requires students to

- Demonstrate the ability to work effectively and respectfully with diverse teams
- Exercise flexibility and willingness to be helpful in making necessary compromises to accomplish a common goal
- Assume shared responsibility for collaborative work, and value the individual contributions made by each team member.

Google contributes to this framework by offering an online environment for creation and sharing, so that students don't have to work on projects alone anymore. The idea of having a group of students standing around while one of them inputs content into Power Point is a thing of the past. Using Google Docs, a group of students can contribute ideas to that same group presentation, but now all of them are working on the project at the same time. By having the students working simultaneously on the same project, it gives all of them the responsibility for the work, with each student having an integral role in the project's completion. Using Google tools for collaborative projects is helping teachers prepare students for the jobs of the 21st century.

Now, getting started with new tools and a shift in your educational philosophy isn't always easy. Many students are used to working on projects by themselves, and teachers are comfortable with assignments being an individual rather than a collective effort. Many teachers are still uncomfortable with the learning curve that technology and web-based tools requires of them. Instructors understand the need to share and work together pedagogically, but often they are still hung up on the technology tools themselves.

Google tools provide one important solution to these technological stumbling blocks. Once teachers start using these tools, they will find them simple to implement and see how effective they are for communicating and collaborating with students. Kids don't have issues adopting new technologies; their only concern is whether or not something works. If a suite of programs like Google tools makes their educational lives easier, they're on board.

■ USING GOOGLE IN THE CLOUD

So, what are the classrooms of tomorrow going to look like? Will students be organized into tidy rows, each working on handouts individually? Or will we see a structure where tables are found throughout the rooms? The future of our classrooms appears to be one-to-one computing, where each student has access to his or her own computing device. Whether that's on an iPod Touch, or a

NetBook isn't the issue; we are going to need to use tools that will function well on a mobile computing device. Google tools offer an effective solution for these smaller computers because files are saved "in the cloud."

Cloud computing means that files are saved through websites, rather than being stored on a local computer's hard drive. Mobile computers don't have the storage space to house a lot of files or programs, so the need to use the cloud is essential. Google Docs, Calendar, Groups, Sites, and Gmail are all housed on the Internet by Google, so files created in these programs will not fill up space on the devices themselves. Making use of cloud computing is a great way to prepare students today for the tools of tomorrow.

What are the advantages of one-to-one computing?

> The America's Digital Schools (ADS) 2008 report identified widespread adoption of one-to-one computing programs and the growing use of online assessments among the key trends in education technology. Of the one-to-one districts surveyed in the report, 78 percent reported "moderate to significant improvement" in student achievement as a result of the program, compared with just 30 percent in 2006. (Dretzin, 2010, n.p.)

When we look at districts across the country working to implement a one-to-one computer initiative for their schools, it becomes even more important to have programs that allow students to work and save files in the cloud of the Internet. Students need to have an easy way to access their projects no matter where they are. We can't expect our students to try and keep track of files on multiple computers or various forms of storage. Most of my students couldn't even remember to bring a pencil to class every day. How can I expect them to remember a flash drive?

As you'll see in the upcoming chapters, one of the biggest advantages of Google tools is the ability to access information from anywhere or any device, as long as you have Internet access. Adopting a suite of programs like Google tools in the classroom will help prepare your students to work in the modern world. It's a simple investment that will yield both short- and long-term gains.

In this section, we're going to look at some specific tools that promote collaboration, communication, and critical thinking: Google Docs, Google Calendar, Gmail, Sites, Blogger, Groups, and we'll introduce Google+. We'll explore how each of these tools can help our students with critical thinking skills and provide teachers with additional avenues for increasing their productivity. As we look at collaboration and communication as crucial 21st century skills, we need to get students beyond the skill-and-drill education of the past and move our instruction into the global information age in which they thrive outside of the classroom.

Google Docs

FIVE THINGS TO KNOW ABOUT GOOGLE DOCS

1. Google Docs consists of documents, spreadsheets, presentations, and forms.
2. You and your students can create documents from scratch or upload existing files.
3. Google Docs provides you with 1 GB of free storage for your files.
4. Collaboration and sharing with Google Docs means you can work whenever with whomever you want.
5. Using forms, you can collect lots of data from students and parents to assist your instruction.

Google Docs has a simple premise, but its impact is revolutionary. The basic idea is this: Rather than creating documents/spreadsheets on one's local computer and sharing them with others via attachments through e-mail, documents are created online and the files are made available by e-mail invitation. Basically, Google Docs provides an online home for documents where people can share their documents by sharing a secure link to others for collaboration.

What does that mean for you and your students? There's only one copy of each document. It lives on the Internet, and students can access it anytime, from anywhere. Before, projects were constantly being moved around and relabeled. Old versions and the latest version of a file were getting mixed up, and there wasn't a clear location for saving the file. Everyone had his or her own solution for this problem, from jump drives, to e-mailing files, to printing hard copies. Even with all those possibilities, the challenge remained, how can I keep track of the different versions of my files, and how can others work on the project concurrently?

Using Google Docs, there is just one home for your projects. This is a safe and secure way to store them, and you control the files. Old versions and new version are stored together. Collaborators can be added as needed. It's up to you.

> **NETS-S Standard 2**
> **Objective a**
> **Communication and Collaboration**
>
> Students use digital media and environments to communicate and work collaboratively, including at a distance, to support individual learning and contribute to the learning of others. Students interact, collaborate, and publish with peers, experts, or others employing a variety of digital environments and media. (ISTE, 2007)

This tool will give students unlimited access to work on their projects. They can work collaboratively with their classmates on group projects, without saving and sending different versions of the project. What does that mean for your classroom workflow? Daily projects like self-starting writing prompts or journals can take place online. Your whole class can brainstorm ideas before class even begins. Projects become more collaborative online, taking less time as part of the actual instruction. Having projects take place as part of homework can actually provide the teacher with more instructional time. Who doesn't want more time?

■ GETTING STARTED IN GOOGLE DOCS

Thus far, we've shared some different ideas surrounding the need to collaborate and communicate in today's schools. Now you're ready to begin your journey in Google Docs.

So, how do you get started? You can find Google Docs in two ways:

1. Go to docs.google.com and enter in your Google account username and password (or set up your Google account if you do not already have one).

2. While you're at google.com, click on the Google menu. It's located in the top left corner of the screen. You'll find **Documents** in the *drop-down menu.*

You've made it. Welcome to Google Docs!

A Few Basics About Google Docs

- All documents, spreadsheets, presentations, and other files are housed in the Library.
- The Library is organized chronologically, with new or recently edited documents displaying at the top of the list.
- All files display in the Library unless they are added to folders.
- Folders display along the left side of the Library.
- Create folders by clicking on the **Create New** button and choosing **Folder.**

Uploading an Existing Document

- Create an online version of an existing file by selecting the **Upload** button along the top left of the Library.
- You'll be directed to a dialog window prompting you to browse to your existing file.
- You can upload documents up to 500 *KB,* spreadsheets up to 1 *MB,* and presentations up to 10 MB in size.

Creating Files in Google Docs

- Create a new file by selecting the **Create New** button.
- You can create several types of files including documents, spreadsheets, presentations, forms, and drawings.
- These options will all be found in a drop-down menu. Choose the right option for your project, and you're on your way.

As we look at the basic tools available to you in Google Docs (see Figure 1.1), you'll find they are very similar to those in Microsoft Word and other word processing programs. All the basic features are present including alignment options, formatting tools, editing controls, and more.

Figure 1.1   Basic Google Docs Tools

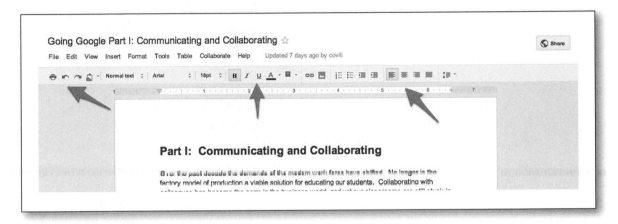

While working on a project, you'll find there's no need to save your work. Google Docs automatically saves your project every time you make a change in your file.

If you would like to work on your project in an offline environment or share it with someone using Microsoft Office, click on the **File** menu and you'll discover a **Download** option to create an offline version of your work.

Most of the getting-started features we've discussed to this point should be fairly familiar to you, as they have similar tools in most standard Microsoft Office programs. Now, let's take a look at some of the features that make Google Docs special. Google Docs makes it possible to do the following:

Sharing

- You can upload files from the entire Microsoft Office suite, or you can create documents from scratch.

Accessing

- Google Docs is available from any computer, as long as you have access to the Internet.

- In addition to the latest draft of a document, Google Docs saves all the previous versions of the project as well.

Storing

- You can store up to 1 GB of documents for free.
- Files can include items from Microsoft Office, PDF files, images, movies, and more.

Communicating

- Google Docs provides users with control over who sees and contributes to a project. You can keep it private or share it with the world.

Let's take a closer look at these features and the skills involved.

■ SHARING

Google Docs allows students and teachers to create or upload documents and share them with others. As the teacher, this gives you several options and strategies. What about a class brainstorming session that happens live with all 30 students contributing their ideas? We do this in class all the time, with kids shouting out their answers. But what happens to the shy student who's a bit more reserved? Brainstorming in a shared document means that everyone's voice gets heard.

Group research projects are a natural fit for Google Docs. It doesn't matter whether it's a document or a presentation—you can have groups of students collaborate on their projects. Students can work on creating the content, and revision can take place throughout the project. Imagine having your students working together through the writing process. They are the ones learning how to evaluate one another's writing. Google Docs provides the tools to make collaborative projects happen (see Figure 1.2).

To invite another person to a Google Doc, you'll want to click on the **Share** button in the upper right-hand corner of any document, spreadsheet, or presentation. Here, you'll be prompted to add collaborators from your contact list, or simply type in a friend's e-mail address and decide what sort of access you wish to provide him or her. He or she can either work on the document as a collaborator, with full editing rights, or the friend can only be allowed to view the document.

As the teacher, you'll want to have your students invite you to their documents as a collaborator, thus giving you the rights to make comments and view changes made to the project in Google Docs.

As the teacher, another huge benefit of being a collaborator on student projects is the ability to review the

Figure 1.2 Sharing Documents With Google Docs

revision history of the document. Located under the File menu, **See revision history** allows the instructor to see how the document has changed over time (see Figure 1.3). For group projects, it also details the contributions of each member of the team. What an asset for managing a group!

Olof Andersson, a middle school teacher from the Kvarnbergsskolan School in Sweden, shared his thoughts about working through the process with his students using Google Docs.

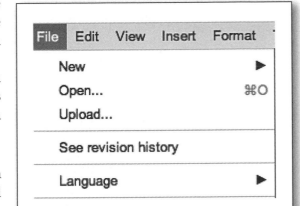

Figure 1.3 See Revision History

> Many of my students use Google Docs when they are working in teams, both with essays and presentations. In some point of progress, the students invite me to join them and have a look at and give comments on their work. It helps me, as a teacher, to be able to participate in the process, not just see the final product. (Google, 2011a)

Beyond collaborating on documents, another aspect of sharing in Google Docs is found in presentations. Students can work on PowerPoint-like presentations in Google Docs. Now there's nothing new about creating a presentation, but here's what is: *Kids can share their presentations online with the rest of the class.* Each student signs in to the online presentation and gets involved in an interactive chat room.

Rather than watching a roomful of bored students sitting through each presentation, now you have students present online. The rest of the class contributes their thoughts about the project in the presentation's chat room. Students become active participants, sharing ideas and contributing to a discussion of the topic. Engagement goes up, and everyone gets involved. As you can see in the example in Figure 1.4, students are actively participating in a presentation by making online comments about the content.

Take the example of Collette Cassinelli (2008), a high school librarian and media teacher from Oregon.

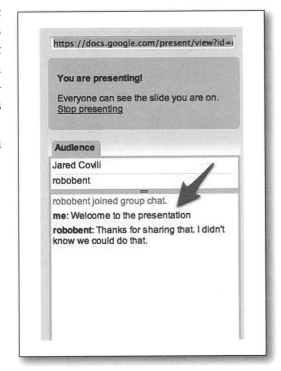

Figure 1.4 Online Chat Area for Students During Presentation

> I have found the REAL POWER of Google Presentations is when you use the **online presentation format.** Instead of my students sitting passively watching a student's PowerPoint presentation, a presenter publishes their presentation online. In the Computer Lab each student logs into a Google account and accesses the presentation URL. I allow students to participate in the chat during the presentation as long as their

comments are about the presentation, they type additional information about the content, or ask questions to the presenter. I monitor the chat closely—but I have to say—when I have done this with my students— there is 100% engagement in the presentation and they handle the responsibility of being in the chat room well (it only takes one student to get kicked out and the rest shape up fast!). They love it and it's a great way to get the whole class involved in a presentation. (n.p.)

Using Templates in Google Docs

If there are two things teachers know how to do well, it's borrowing and sharing. We are willing to share lessons and handouts we've made with our colleagues, and we don't mind using their resources either. Most of us are so busy trying to get through with all the demands of teaching that when a good resource presents itself, we're all over it.

Google Docs has a library containing educational documents, spreadsheets, and presentations. The Template Gallery is full of useful resources for teachers and students. Instructors can find everything from grade book programs to attendance summaries for classroom management. There are lesson plan *templates* to assist you in creating future activities. Students can find many types of productivity aids including note-taking templates, science reports, and term paper structures. Think of it as an entire portfolio of free resources, shared by teachers and students for their peers.

To access the template gallery, you'll find a **From Template** option under the **Create New** menu (see Figure 1.5). Your other options are to **Browse Template Gallery** across the top of your Library, or try searching the template gallery using the provided link. If you create a document you'd like to share with the gallery, choose the **Submit a Template** link from the template gallery and it will become available to other users. The Template Gallery is a wonderful place to find and share some of our best ideas.

Figure 1.5   Finding Templates in Google Docs

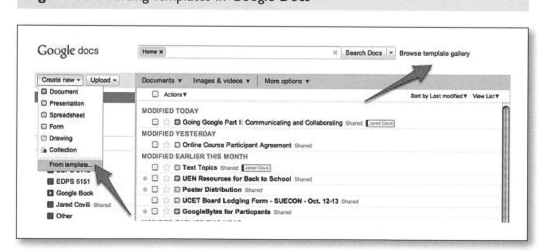

ACCESSING ■

Students are no longer bound to a location when working on a project. If you have Internet access, you can work on a Google Doc. What a great solution for students working on a project from school and at home. They can simply pick up right where they left off because Google Docs has saved a copy of their project, just as they left it! This may not seem like that big a deal to some of your students, but wait until they experience the dreaded "computer crash." As an example, take the experience Julie Meloni (2009) had with one of her students.

> "All your documents are backed up," I said to them, but this didn't hit home until one student ran into class one day and said, "Oh my gosh, my computer died in the middle of my essay!" I calmly opened my laptop, logged into my account (as I was a collaborator on the document), and showed the student the essay—saved constantly by Google until her computer crashed. It was at that moment that 24 light bulbs appeared over students' heads and any lingering resistance to the technology vanished. (n.p.)

As a teacher, your access to students and their work increases dramatically as well. Gone are the days of searching through an endless number of drafts. Once students share their projects with you, you can look through the single copy of the document and find all the changes with one click. What's more, you can manage all of the work in a paperless environment! Student projects can easily be organized into online folders, so managing documents is a snap.

Never Buy Software Again!

Google Docs also makes moot the debate as to which format to have student use to save their documents. It doesn't matter which software they have on their home computer. Since Google Docs is an online set of tools, you and your students don't even need to have Microsoft Office. As long as they have the Internet they have access to their files on Google Docs.

Since Google Docs is a free tool, this can be part of a school- or districtwide technology plan. Imagine the savings to our financially challenged schools when they stop buying software and use that money elsewhere. As one teacher commented, "I guess I really don't need to have Microsoft Word anymore. As long as I have the Internet, I can use Google Docs."

STORING ■

Google Docs might just remedy the eternal student declaration, "The dog ate my homework." No longer will students lose their projects between home and school. Now, all their files will be in one location, easy to access and share. Google provides users with 1 *GB*, or gigabyte, of free online storage, meaning you can probably store every document, spreadsheet, and presentation you own for free!

Figure 1.6   Use Folders to Manage Files

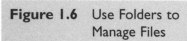

- ▼ My folders
  - ▶ 📁 EDPS 5151
  - ▶ 📁 Google Chrome
  - ▶ 📁 Other
  - ▶ 📁 UCET
- ▶ Folders shared with me

In addition to being able to store documents, spreadsheets, and presentations, Google Docs also allows users to store other files like PDFs, images, videos, and so forth. This gives you additional options, but remember, the more multimedia files you include, the quicker your storage space gets filled. If you need to increase your storage, Google provides a cheap solution. For $5 a year, you can expand your storage from 1 GB to 20 GB.

Previously, I mentioned that you can create folders in Google Docs as storage for your files. This is another nice aspect of the program—it can become your personal filing cabinet, online (see Figure 1.6). While this may seem unnecessary as you begin using Google Docs, over time you'll continue to amass more and more files until it can become very overwhelming. Remember, a little file management in the beginning can save you huge headaches in the long run. Folders are an easy way to store your documents and find them later!

■ COMMUNICATING

Google Docs provides you with several ways to communicate with parents and students. We've already explored how you can share documents, spreadsheets, and presentations with individuals, but you can also make files public and share them with everyone else. What a great way to publicize your classroom newsletter or share your disclosure document!

While getting your message out is important, it may be even more vital to get the students' and parents' *opinions*. Remember, students and their parents are your main clients. If you aren't in touch with their desires and needs, you may be setting yourself up for unnecessary challenges. One of my favorite components in Google Docs is the Forms feature, which can be used to get authentic feedback from the people who matter most. As with the other tools in Google Docs, it's easy to share a form—you can either e-mail it out to people or make it public and share the link.

The power isn't so much in the form itself, but in your ability to take the information gained and plan your teaching strategy accordingly. Most kids want their opinions to be heard, but few feel comfortable sharing verbally with the teacher. The Forms function allows individuals to give their input and provides the teacher with an easy way to access the feedback.

Project Idea: Student Writing Group

As a former Language Arts teacher, I think Google Docs is an incredibly effective solution for student writing groups. Here's why. As our students work through various drafts of a research project, many of us have the students engage in some type of peer review. This helps the writer get feedback on what's working and what isn't going as well. Peer review also helps the reviewers, as they see some of the mistakes they're making in their own writing as they evaluate another paper.

Setting Up a Peer-Reviewed Paper

Have the author create the document using the **Create New** button and selecting **Document.** The author of the document needs to "share" the project with the rest of the peer reviewers. Once the author uses the **Share** button, he or she will be prompted for the e-mail addresses of the peer reviewers.

One management strategy I like involves using the **Comments** feature (see Figure 1.7). Found in the Insert menu, Comments provides peer reviewers with an easy spot to make suggestions without deleting any of the original work. If you have more than one peer reviewer, have the students pick a specific font color to use when they make their own comments.

Once the author reviews the comments made by their peers, he or she can take those comments and make future revisions. Using the revision history, the student can compare various versions of the paper and see the progress he or she has made.

To help students work through the revision process together, I would suggest not asking to be added as a collaborator until the students are a good distance into the project. Too often, once the instructor becomes part of the process, the other reviewers tend to defer to the teacher. Refrain from joining the project to begin with, and let the students work through the process.

Using the **Revision History** is a good management strategy for you as the instructor. Once you are added to the document, you can quickly assess the work of each student, not just the author. Because the revision history keeps track of each change on a document, you can see what contributions each reviewer has made. This illustrates to the students that each of their comments is observed and that everyone contributes to the success of a project.

As the time comes for the final draft to be submitted, the nice part for teachers is they already have access to the document. Now it's time to move the file from the Library into a final versions folder. You can create a folder that gets placed along the left side of the Google Docs library. Folders can be set up for different subjects, class periods, or however you want.

Working in student writing groups uses several different elements of sharing, revising, and evaluating. Google Docs provides the structure and the support to help students work through any peer-reviewed project.

NETS-S Standard 2 Objective d

Students use digital media and environments to communicate and work collaboratively, including at a distance, to support individual learning and contribute to the learning of others. Students contribute to project teams to produce original works or solve problems. (ISTE, 2007)

Figure 1.7 Comments Help With Revision

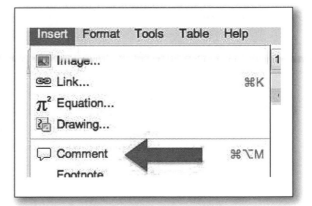

Project Idea: Creating a Parent Contact Form

NETS-T Standard 3 Objective b

Teachers collaborate with students, peers, parents, and community members using digital tools and resources to support student success and innovation (ISTE, 2008).

One of the first things a teacher needs from his or her students at the beginning of the school year is contact information for parents or guardians. We want to know whom we can contact, where, when, and how. Sure, the school can provide us with a lot of this information, but much of it is out of date or just incorrect, and it requires us going through the administration to access the data. Creating a Google form is an easy solution to this beginning-of-school-year problem. Here's how to get started (see Figures 1.8 and 1.9).

Figure 1.8   Creating a New Form

Creating the Form

- Select **Create New** from the button along the top left side of the Google Doc library and drop down to **Form.**
- As soon as you start a form, you'll find it has a basic structure: name the form, provide instructions, ask questions.
- For our sample project, you'll need to name your form something like "Parent Contact Form."
- Following the title, in the **instructions** field, be sure to provide a basic overview of what information you'd like from parents and how you plan to use that information in the future.
- Next we'll start creating the basic **questions** we need for our form (see Figure 1.9). Note: The default type of question in a Google form is text (see Figure 1.10). Simply put, you want your respondent to enter his or her answers manually. So, we need to

Figure 1.9   Setting up a Form

| Add Item ▾ | Theme: Plain | | Email this form | See responses ▾ | More actions ▾ | Save |

Untitled form

You can include any text or info that will help people fill this out.

Question Title	Sample Question 1
Help Text	
Question Type	Text ▾

Their answer

(Done) ☐ Make this a required question

create basic text questions that will provide us with important contact information about our students' parents. Examples of text questions may include Parent Name, Student Name, or Parent Contact Number. To enter in this data, you'll simply type
in the **Question Title** for what you'd like to know. For example, if I'd like to know the parent's name, I'll enter that in the Question Title.

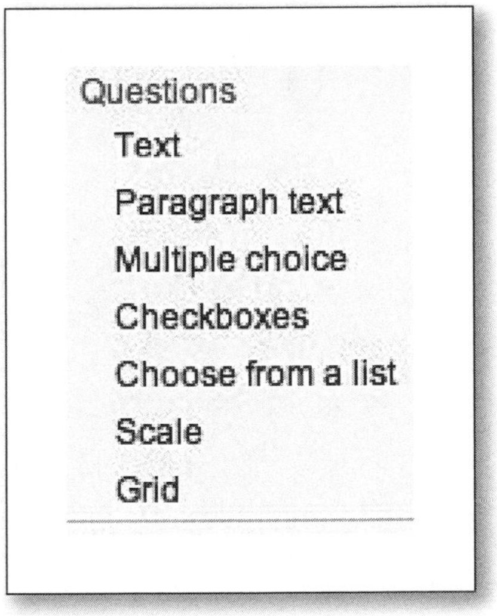

Figure 1.10   Question Types

Questions
   Text
   Paragraph text
   Multiple choice
   Checkboxes
   Choose from a list
   Scale
   Grid

There are a few additional aspects to each question in a form. Google provides a space for clarifying information. This is called **Help Text.** For our form, it probably isn't necessary, but it can be useful to ensure you get the data you need. After Help Text, you'll see a space to choose your **Question Type.** I mentioned that the default style of question is text, but there are several types of questions at your disposal. Currently the list includes Text, Paragraph Text, Multiple Choice, Checkboxes, Choose from a list, Scale, and Grid. Each one of these options can be useful for gathering specific types of data.

The final option in creating a question is whether or not to **require the answer.** This means a form cannot be submitted without a reply to that question (see Figure 1.11). For our example, items like Student Name, Parent Name, and Phone Number or E-mail are essential to the success of our project. These items would definitely be required before someone could hit submit.

Figure 1.11   Required Questions

☐ **Make this a required question**

Adding Additional Questions

When you first create a form, you'll find that two sample text-style questions automatically populate the fields. If you want to add additional questions, look in the top left corner of the form and you'll find the **Add a Question** button. This is a drop-down menu that allows you to select from the options mentioned previously (i.e., Checkboxes, Scale, etc.).

Editing a Question

Once you've established a field of data, changing it doesn't require starting over. Instead, you just need to do the following (see Figure 1.12):

- On the right side of each question, you'll find three editing buttons. Use the pencil icon to edit a question, an overlapping box icon to copy a question, or a trash can icon to delete the question.
- The pencil icon reopens the question in edit mode. Here you can change the wording of your question, add more options, or even change the style of question.

Figure 1.12   Editing a Question

- The overlapping box is useful if you have a series of similarly formatted questions. Simply duplicate the question, and make the minor adjustments you need without retyping the entire field. A great example of this would be during a multiple-choice quiz. Perhaps two or three of the questions have the same options for answers. Rather than retype the five or six answer choices, simply copy and paste the entire entry and adjust the question, leaving the answers intact. This can save quite a bit of time.
- We all have a pretty good idea that clicking on the trash can will delete the selected question. When you're finished with your changes, click on the Done button and you're all set.

Sharing the Form With Parents

So, you've put the final touches on your form and you're ready to get parents to respond. Now what? You have a couple of different choices.

1. You could use the **Share** button and enter in all the parents' e-mail addresses so you can send the form directly to them. One problem: You need the e-mail addresses, which is why you made the form in the first place. Here's a better choice.

2. At the bottom of every form is a public URL (see Figure 1.13). The *URL* is a site's address on the web. This one is a long, ugly address, but we've got a nice solution to work around that issue. There's a great website from Google found at http://goo.gl, which allows you to transform a nasty very long URL like https://spreadsheets0.google.com/viewform?formkey=dDZKdzlZOXpBYWhFQlcxOFlDRk16QWc6MQ into an easy-to-use URL, http::://goo.gl/T3DE5y

Now that you've created a usable address for parents to find the form, your next job is to market it. How do you get this form into the hands of the parents?

- Perhaps you could include the address to your form in your disclosure document, distributed on Back to School Night or during the first week of class.

Figure 1.13 Public URL for Form

Which Days are best for you to Co Op? *
◯ Monday

You can view the published form here: https://spreadsheets1.google.com/viewform?formkey=dDZUOU1BQXFWa2dzamJlSEhybHE1VFE6MQ

- Another good option is to add the web link to your classroom website (if you don't have a website yet, we'll get to that shortly).

Once the parents start filling out the form, the final question is, where do the answers go? Here's the beauty of Google Docs. When you created the form, Google Docs created a spreadsheet for the answers. When you go back to your Google Docs Library, you'll find there's already a spreadsheet with all of your data fields ready for responses.

If you want to edit the form or use any of its data, click on the Form option in the menus and you'll have a variety of choices (see Figure 1.14). You can end submissions, summarize the data, edit the form, and more. It's a great system, and an easy way to organize the information you need to start the year off right.

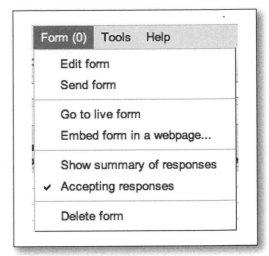

Figure 1.14 Working With a Form

Project Idea: Creating Online Quizzes

Assessment is such a major part of your classroom. Using Google Docs, you can create a form that will help you uncover student understanding and compile the data in an easy-to-use spreadsheet.

As we've learned about Google Forms, creating an online quiz is as simple as developing a series of questions you want to ask your students. Remember, there are several different types of questions, so you can write the questions to look at many kinds of data. Whether you want to use multiple choice or a paragraph response, it's up to you.

The key for assessment is being able to use the answers to quickly identify student comprehension or identify teaching areas that need improvement. Once the quiz is completed, all student responses are submitted into a spreadsheet that allows you to compile the data in many useful ways.

One of the best ways to analyze the data is to create a **Summary of Responses.** With this option, you can view a chart representing the various responses. For a quick formative assessment, this is a lifesaver. Within seconds of the quiz ending, a teacher can see how the class performed as a whole. It's an easy way to view what your students are thinking and determine where you need to spend your instructional time. In the Figure 1.15 example below, you'll see how easy it is to find out what students are thinking and learning.

Another useful option for scoring your quiz is the script called **Flubaroo.** I know it's a funny name, but it works great. Flubaroo is found in the **Insert** menu, under the **script** option. Just type the word "Flubaroo" in the search box, and you'll find it. Once you install the script, you'll find that Flubaroo has an

Figure 1.15 See Quick Data With Summary of Responses

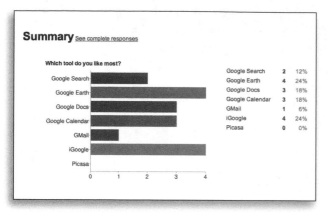

option in your text menus across the top of your Google Spreadsheet. Click on this menu option to get started.

Setup is easy, as Flubaroo runs a little wizard to help you install the script. Please note: You have to set up Flubaroo for each new quiz you create. As you run the wizard you'll find that Flubaroo wants to use one of the submissions as the answer key, so you'll either have to take the quiz yourself or use one of the students (provided they get all of the answers correct).

With the answer key established, Flubaroo will quickly score all of the quizzes and provide you with a detailed summary of each student's score. Hint: Be sure to include a question on the quiz that requires an e-mail address. You can then use the e-mail address to send students their scores. This is an option in the Flubaroo menu.

I've shared some of my favorite projects over the past few pages, but one of the best things about this tool is the ways in which you'll use it. There is more than one right way to encourage students to communicate and collaborate with one another. The most important part of any tool is how it helps you and your students achieve your learning goals.

MORE IDEAS FOR GOING GOOGLE

Other Google Docs Projects

- Creating word searches, flash cards, QR (quick response) code scavenger hunts, and more. Use the Gadgets option under the Insert menu in your Google Spreadsheets. You can search for tons of fun little applications in Gadgets.
- Developing an online writing portfolio for students
- Creating a Choose Your Own Adventure presentation for students.
- Brainstorming a class activity or learning topic using an open spreadsheet.
- Developing a classroom newsletter
- Creating an online checkout list for classroom books.

TIPS FOR THE GOOGLE CLASSROOM

- Make sure all of your students have Google accounts for smoother sharing. Many students will already have an account, but you'll want to make sure you help those that don't currently have access.
- Google Docs is only one of the tools Google offers for the classroom. Look at how the tool can play a part in your overall teaching strategy.
- Start small by having your students work collaboratively with one other student. Don't try to tackle whole-class projects right at the beginning. Be patient!

2

Google Calendar

◈◈

FIVE THINGS TO KNOW ABOUT GOOGLE CALENDAR

1. Calendars can be shared among multiple people.
2. Calendars can be public or private.
3. You can own or contribute to multiple calendars.
4. Calendars can be embedded in your website.
5. Parents and students can subscribe to your classroom calendar.

◈◈

As we look at our hectic lives, many of us would be lost without some type of planner, calendar, or notebook. We jot down events and plans into our three-ring binders, knowing that we rely upon these books to keep us on time and focused. Whether it's for our personal or professional lives, a calendar is our essential system for maintaining our schedules.

One of the most important communication tools a teacher has to share with parents is the classroom calendar. Over the years, there have been several different methods used by teachers for sharing important dates and events. For years, teachers have created a classroom newsletter with a one-page calendar included that covers the next 30 days. This has been a useful system for presenting information, but it is soon out of date and is easy to misplace. As we moved into the digital age, a teacher's webpage became a perfect place to share an electronic version of the schedule. This was and is a great way to share information, but many websites are difficult to update, and the calendar can be easily neglected as a result.

Google has developed a calendar tool that is easy to use. It doesn't require any knowledge of web design and there are no special programs to purchase. The calendar is dynamic, and it can be updated instantly to share information with parents and students. It can be easily shared, so parents and students don't have to hunt around the web to find the events that are important to your class. Let's learn more about Google Calendar.

> **NETS-T Standard 3 and Objective C**
>
> Teachers exhibit knowledge, skills, and work processes representative of an innovative professional in a global and digital society. Teachers communicate relevant information and ideas effectively to students, parents, and peers using a variety of digital-age media and formats. (ISTE, 2008)

25

■ GETTING STARTED WITH GOOGLE CALENDAR

To create a Google Calendar, you need to use your Google account. Once you have your account, you'll find Google Calendar in one of two ways:

1. Go to www.google.com/calendar and enter your Google account username and password.

2. Or, while you're on google.com, click on the **Google** icon in the top left corner of the screen. At the bottom of the drop-down list, click on **More** link. You'll find **Calendar** among the options that pop up.

By default, Google will want you to create a personal account with your first and last name as the calendar's name. This is automatic and something you'll want to let occur. Still, a personal calendar isn't something you'll want to share with others, so let's go through the process of creating your classroom calendar.

■ CREATING A CLASSROOM CALENDAR

Your classroom calendar is going to be a public calendar you can share with parents and students. You should only plan on including events that everyone can see and that relate to assignments and activities associated with school. To create a new calendar,

1. Click on the drop-down menu next to the **My Calendars** menu along the left side of the screen.

2. Choose **Create New Calendar.** You'll find yourself on the **Calendar Details** page.

3. Basic settings for your new calendar include **Calendar Name, Description,** and **Location** (see Figure 2.1). These elements should provide enough

Figure 2.1 Calendar Settings

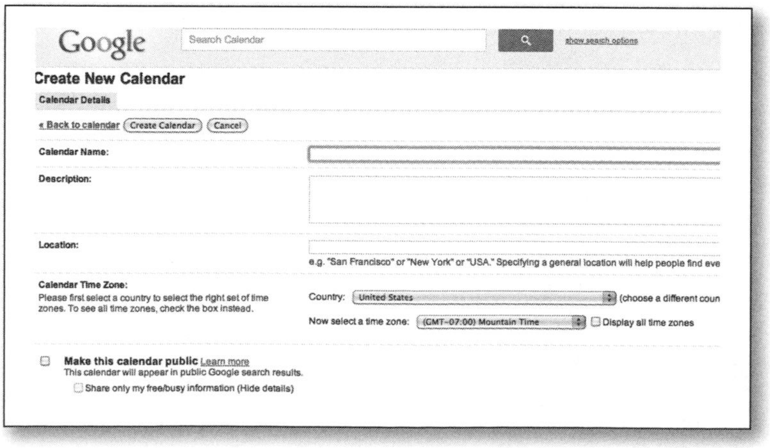

information to enable parents and students to find your calendar, but you still want to keep all the information strictly related to your classroom.

    a. Calendar Name: The name of your calendar will appear in any Google searches for your events and information. This means if someone types "Mr. Covili's Classroom Calendar" into the calendar search box, he or she will be able to find my specific calendar.

    b. Description: A brief description will help you ensure that your calendar finds its target audience. This doesn't need to be more than a line or two, but it provides that extra information to help parents.

    c. Location: As with the description, including a location helps parents to make sure they have the correct Mr. Smith. Including the name of your school is a good way to make this happen.

4. Once you've filled in all of the Calendar Details, you have the option to make your calendar **public.** Your school calendar will need to be public in order to help parents and students find it. If this calendar is private, the only way for parents to access it is through direct contact with you. While that may be "safer" and keep the information more private, it really hinders interested parties from finding your school calendar. We want this calendar to be accessible to more parents, and making it public is a good way to help this happen.

5. The last step is to save all of your information for the new calendar. To do this, click on the **Create Calendar** button along the top or bottom of the screen. That's it; you've just created your new classroom calendar!

ADDING EVENTS AND MANAGING ■
YOUR CLASSROOM CALENDAR

Now that you've created your calendar, it's time to start adding content to share with parents and students. Google Calendar makes this as simple as clicking and typing. Here are the basic steps:

Figure 2.2 Creating a New Event

1. Click on the calendar on the appropriate date and time for your selected event. This will create a new 1-hour event.

2. When you first create the event, the only requested information is the *What,* or the event's title.

3. Since you have both a personal and classroom calendar, you'll want to use the drop-down menu to select the appropriate calendar.

4. To add information to an event on your calendar, click on the existing event. Select the option to **Edit event details.**

5. On this screen, you can add or edit several pieces of information including the name of the event, the date and time of the event, the length of the event, a description of the event, the location of the event, privacy settings, and any specific guests.

6. Once you complete the event, be sure to click **Save** along the left side of the screen. You can now go **Back to calendar.**

Your updated event is now displayed on the calendar.

Event Basics

- Creating All-Day Events: Click in the area without a specific time at the top of each day.
- Creating Repeat events: Use the radio button in the Edit Event settings to have an event repeat. You can choose from option such as repeating Daily, Weekly, Monthly, or Yearly.
- Changing the day or time of an event: Simply click on the event you wish to change, and drag it to the correct day or time. If you click on the bottom of an event, you can drag out the time (i.e., you can lengthen an event beyond 1 hour).

■ WHY USE GOOGLE CALENDAR?

Many of us already have a calendar system we use and love, so why would we want to switch to Google Calendar? A big reason to create your classroom calendar in Google Calendar has to do with communicating. A paper classroom planner is personal and can't be shared with others. The same thing holds true for calendars on Outlook or Groupwise. These are great tools for individual use, but they don't help parents and students find out about classroom events. Your Google Calendar can be shared with anyone you want, making it a terrific system for spreading the word about the great things going on in your classroom.

Since your calendar is online and public, another big advantage to parents and students lies in the diverse methods in which they can access the information. Each Google Calendar can have a public URL, giving users the chance to bookmark a link to the teacher's calendar. This works, but there's an even better option for most parents and students.

With the average online classroom calendar, the only place to access the information is from the teacher's website. The problem is, most of us don't check a classroom website on a daily basis. Information gets missed and is often overlooked. Rather than going out for information, Google Calendar brings the information to you. Here's how it works.

■ SUBSCRIBING TO A CLASSROOM CALENDAR

Once a calendar is made public, it has a unique URL. Anyone with that address can access the calendar online. In the past, this is the address most of us would have bookmarked, never to be seen again amongst the virtual pile of "favorite" websites. With Google Calendar, instead of bookmarking, you "subscribe" to any public calendar. This means the events from that calendar show up on your own Google Calendar. Here are two ways to subscribe to a Google Calendar.

One way for parents to subscribe to your calendar is to type your e-mail address in the search box under the **Other calendars** heading (see Figure 2.3). This means you'll want to provide parents with your Google account e-mail. Most likely, this is your Gmail account address.

Once parents add your public calendar to their list, it will display in the **Other calendars** section of their Google Calendar account. Even though your classroom calendar is public, the default sharing setting is "view only," meaning they cannot change anything on it.

Another option for adding your classroom calendar involves visiting the calendar online and subscribing directly. Here's how this works. When parents and students visit the URL of your calendar, they will find a **Subscribe** button in the lower right corner of the calendar. Hitting this button will add your classroom calendar to the subscriber's Google Calendar account under the **Other calendars** section (see Figure 2.4).

As with the other method for subscribing, using the + **Google Calendar** button provides the person with view status of your classroom calendar. They do not have privileges to edit or add events to the calendar.

Figure 2.3 Subscribe to a Calendar With an E-mail Address

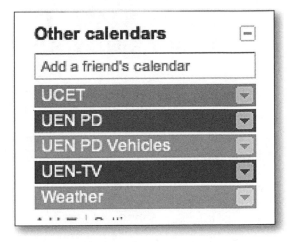

Figure 2.4 Subscription Button on Classroom Calendar

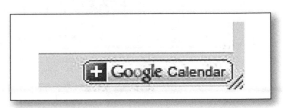

GOOGLE CALENDAR AND THE CLOUD ■

We've already discussed how the cloud provides better access to our information online. Since Google Calendar lives in the cloud, we can have access to our calendar from any computer or device with Internet access. This makes it easy to update events from school or from home. It also means that our calendar can be accessed on several different devices, both desktop and mobile.

Here, Google (2011e) describes the advantage of having your data in the cloud:

Data is stored in the cloud—not on one particular computer—so [users] can connect with all of their information and get work done from any Internet connection. Google's infrastructure gives users seamless access to their information at work, at home, on the road and from their mobile devices. With traditional technology, important information can be trapped in software only available on a limited set of devices, preventing [users] from being their most productive. (n.p.)

Having access to your calendar in the cloud not only provides you with more options to update and share events, it also means that parents and students can access your events from their mobile devices. Anytime you can share data to someone's cell phone, your chance of the person seeing the information increases.

■ SHARING YOUR GOOGLE CALENDAR

Figure 2.5 Accessing the Sharing Settings

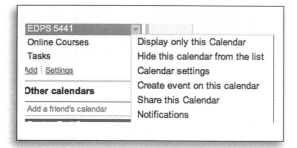

Google Calendar is a wonderful tool to use for communicating with others, but what about using it to collaborate? Google Calendar is useful for departmental calendars, the school website, or club calendars. One nice thing is that, since it exists as part of the cloud, multiple individuals can add and manage events on the same calendar. Here are the steps to share your Google Calendar with collaborators (see Figure 2.5):

1. Go to your list of **My Calendars** (in the menu along the left side of your calendar display).

2. Click on the drop-down menu for your calendar.

3. Select the option to **Share this Calendar.**

4. Under the option to **Share** with specific people, you'll find a window to type in someone's e-mail address. To add a collaborator to your calendar, you'll need the person's e-mail address.

5. Once you've entered the e-mail address, the next step is to select the **Permission** settings for that person. You've got four choices to pick from (see Figure 2.6):

Figure 2.6 Sharing Setting Options

Make changes AND manage sharing
Make changes to events
✓ See all event details
See only free/busy (hide details)

a. Make changes and manage sharing: This enables the person to add/edit events, but it also gives him or her the right to share the calendar with others.
b. Make changes to events: This gives the ability to add and edit events.
c. See all event details: This provides user access to view events on the calendar.
d. See only free/busy (hide details): Viewer can only see blocked out times for events, with no other details.

Project Idea: Adding Your Calendar to Your Website

Many of you have a classroom website you've spent hours creating. In the past, one of the hardest things to update on your site was the calendar page. No more. Rather than recreate your Google Calendar for your website, you can simply embed it. The best part is that once your calendar is embedded in your school website, any new events you create are automatically found on both versions of the calendar. Let's set this up.

1. Find your classroom calendar in the **My Calendars** menu (along the left side of your calendar display).

2. Click on the drop-down menu along the right side of the calendar.

3. Select **Calendar Settings** from the menu.

4. You'll find yourself on the Calendar Details page for your classroom calendar. Look toward the bottom of the page for the heading **Embed this Calendar**.

Figure 2.7 Embed Code for Calendar

Embedding a calendar requires copying some *HTML embed code* and pasting it onto a page on your classroom website (see Figure 2.7). Before you copy the code, however, you have the option to customize the code to make it work on your site. Let's look at a couple of useful choices (see Figure 2.8).

Perhaps the most important element you'll want to customize on your calendar is the size. Depending on the pixel dimensions of your classroom website, you may need to adjust the width and height of your calendar before you embed it in your site.

Size also plays a part in the default view you choose for your calendar. Most teachers use the month view since it's the default choice. The problem is that the calendar view doesn't give you much information because the individual days are fairly limited in size. Try choosing **Agenda View,** and see how it displays more details about a specific event.

Figure 2.8 Customizing Your Calendar for Embedding

Another key option for your calendar is selecting the correct calendars. You'll find that if you have several different calendars, you can pick and choose which calendar you wish to display on your site. Why is this important? If you're a secondary school teacher, you may have created a calendar for each class you teach. Rather than display events for different preps, you can choose to only include the event for a specific calendar.

Figure 2.9 Copy the HTML Code for Your Calendar

```
<iframe src="http://www.google.com/calendar/embed?
src=1om1pjb7m36et5pa6q4dl0eco0%40group.calendar.g
oogle.com&ctz=America/Denver" style="border: 0"
width="800" height="600" frameborder="0" scrolling="no">
</iframe>
```

Once you finish customizing the code, be sure to use the **Update HTML** option to save the changes.

Now that you've customized your calendar you'll want to copy all HTML code in the window (see Figure 2.9).

Once you arrive at your website, you'll need to paste the code on the appropriate page for your site. If you're using Dreamweaver, be sure to paste your selected code into the Code View of your page. If you're using Blogger, Weebly, or most online web creation tools, look for a *gadget* that accepts HTML code. (A gadget is an element of a blog or website that can be customized. It will be discussed more fully later in the text.)

Paste your code, and you're done!

As you've seen in this section, Google Calendar is easy to set up and share with others. It's a great way to provide information about the events of your classroom and an effective collaborative tool to use with colleagues. The hardest part of using this system is staying up to date and being organized on your end. All you have to do is know your schedule; Google Calendar makes everything else happen.

MORE IDEAS FOR GOING GOOGLE

Possible Google Calendars for School

- Use Google Calendar to create the calendar for all school events. You can enter everything from sporting events to the lunch menu on a given day.
- Create a signup calendar for shared school spaces like the computer lab or library. This can be an easy way to let teachers know if these "prime" spaces are available on a given day.
- Use Google Calendar to show your available or busy times during Parent Teacher Conferences. Using **Appointment Slots,** you can actually have parents schedule their appointment with you.
- Create a department calendar to share materials with your fellow teachers (i.e., books, SmartBoard, projector, etc).

TIPS FOR THE GOOGLE CLASSROOM

- Parents and students don't need to have a Gmail account in order to view a Google Calendar. However, if individuals want to subscribe to a Google Calendar, Google will prompt them to create an account so they can subscribe it.
- Once events are created in the calendar, they are permanently saved. This means you can go back to events and update from year to year if you continue to follow the same basic classroom schedule. This can be a huge timesaver once the events are created.
- As you create events, add more details in the description field. It's much easier for parents and students to understand, "Today's test covers Chapter 11 in your textbook" than simply, "Big Test Today."

3

Gmail

FIVE THINGS TO KNOW ABOUT GMAIL

1. Gmail provides you with 7 GB of storage for your account.
2. Gmail groups messages into threaded conversations, making it easier to follow a discussion.
3. Gmail incorporates instant chat and video chat to improve personal communication.
4. Gmail uses Google search technology and has an effective spam filter.
5. Gmail can import contacts and forward messages, making your transition from other mail programs simple.

For most of us, e-mail is one of the best ways for us to stay in touch with everyone. Think about the way most of us start our workday. As soon as the computer is up, most of us open up our e-mail to see what messages are waiting for us. E-mail is the primary communication tool between parents and teachers. Even if students may say "email is for old people" (Anderson, 2006), it is still the most common way for teachers to communicate with students. Why?

E-mail is a great way for teachers to communicate with parents and students in a documented format. If you have concerns with grades or performance, e-mail is an effective method of sharing those issues. It creates a "paper trail" and can be a useful way to ensure that information is "on the record."

E-mail also allows us to communicate with several people at once. You can send messages to select groups of students or to your entire class. It provides a quick way to get your message out to everyone who needs it. Gmail provides teachers with a practical way to communicate—there's a reason it was the first tool created by Google!

> **NETS-T Standard 3 and Objective b**
>
> Teachers exhibit knowledge, skills, and work processes representative of an innovative professional in a global and digital society. Teachers collaborate with students, peers, parents, and community members using digital tools and resources to support student success and innovation. (ISTE, 2008)

■ GETTING STARTED WITH GMAIL

Figure 3.1 Creating a Gmail Account

New to Gmail? It's free and easy.

Create an account »

About Gmail   New features!

Earlier in the book, we talked about the need to create a Gmail account when you first start using Google tools. *Please note: If you created a Google account using an e-mail account other than Gmail, your login will change the instant you create a Gmail address.* I know this seems a bit proprietary, but I think it makes things simpler in the long run. For all your Google tools, the login will be your Gmail address. In case you still need to create your Gmail account, let's look at how this is done (see Figure 3.1).

1. Access Gmail at mail.google.com. You can also find a link to Gmail along the top left side of the Google homepage.

2. Here you'll be prompted to log in with your account and password. Since you don't have this information, you'll find a large button beneath the login window inviting you to **Create an account.**

Figure 3.2 Choosing a Username and Password

Get started with Gmail

First name:

Last name:

Desired Login Name: @gmail.com
    Examples: JSmith, John.Smith
    (check availability!)

Choose a password: ••••••••   Password strength:
    Minimum of 8 characters in
    length.

3. The most important part of creating your Gmail account is twofold: picking a username and a password (see Figure 3.2). The username has to be something unique, and with several million Gmail accounts in use, this can be pretty tricky.

    Also, since you're going to be using this account as part of your classroom, you'll want to ensure you pick something that's not a distraction. I'd suggest creating a username that implies you're a teacher—i.e., coviliclassroom or mrcovili. You might have to be a bit more creative than that, but you get the idea.

Selecting a password is something we're all getting used to in the Internet age. Google will help you in choosing a password that is the most secure.

As you type in the letters and numbers, Google will indicate how secure the password is with a security strength meter. Remember to keep track of your username and password—but try not to write it down on a Post-it note and stick it to your computer!

GMAIL BASICS

As with other e-mail programs, the basic functionality you're looking for is to send and receive messages. You want to be able to organize your messages into categories. You want the ability to attach files, both large and small. These are the things you expect an e-mail client to do; Gmail does all these things and more.

Here are a few of Gmail's available tools:

*   Composing mail—To create a new message, click on the **Compose Mail** button along the top left of the Gmail screen (see Figure 3.3).

- Attaching a file—Gmail allows you to attach files up to 20 MB in size. This is considerably larger than your average e-mail client. If a student wants to send you an assignment, 20 MB allows him or her the space to send various types of files. You can even send relatively small videos and photos!
- Organizing e-mail—Gmail organizes your e-mails a bit differently than most traditional e-mail clients. Here are some of the major differences:

Figure 3.3 Compose Mail Button

  o Threaded conversations: Rather than e-mails simply being placed in your inbox chronologically, Gmail keeps conversations (replies to an e-mail thread) together. You don't have to search through your inbox to figure out how someone's comments or questions relate in an old message. It takes a few tries at this to get used to this new way of organizing messages, but most find this feature really helps them to keep up with an ongoing conversation.
  o Priority Inbox: This is a fairly new feature in Gmail. Google keeps track of your most important contacts and messages and moves them into the Priority Inbox (It does this by determining which mail comes from listservs or other commercial entities and which comes from individual senders.). When parents, students, and colleagues e-mail you, the messages will go into the Priority Inbox instead of getting mixed in with the rest of your messages. It's a convenient way to keep track of your most important messages.
  o Applying labels: This is a major departure from Outlook and other traditional e-mail clients. Rather than organizing messages into specific folders, Gmail has you apply labels to messages. Your labels are color coded so you can set up different colors for various types of messages. You can set up specific labels for parents, colleagues, and students. If you teach in a secondary school, you may want to set up labels for your individual preps or for each period of the day. Once labels are applied to messages, you can sort for the specific labels, or messages can be moved out of the inbox and into the labeled folder.

- Searching messages: Gmail utilizes Google's superior search technology to help you find e-mails. How often do you know there is a certain message in your inbox but you can't find it among the rest of your mail? Using the search box in Gmail, you can look for names, addresses, keywords, and more to help you find those "lost" messages.

ADVANTAGES OF USING GMAIL ■

So let's say you're comfortable using Outlook. Why would you want to use Gmail? I can't say that you should completely abandon whichever e-mail service your school is currently using (I'd rather argue that your school/district should make the switch for everyone, but we'll talk about that later). For now, here are some of the "pros" of using Gmail as your main e-mail client.

Storage

We all want more room when it comes to saving our messages and their attachments. Gmail has over 7 GB of storage available, meaning you'll probably never get the dreaded *"Mailbox has exceeded its allotted storage amount"* message again. Add this to the 20 MB attachment size limit, and you can see why Gmail has all the storage you could want.

For students, extra storage can help eliminate the issues of losing files due to lack of allocated space. It also gives them an additional backup for any projects they're working on while at school.

Spam Filter

No one wants to get advertisement e-mails or spam in their inbox. Most of us spend a lot of time trying to create filters to eliminate unwanted solicitations and junk mail. At the same time, we can't run the risk of important e-mails accidentally getting the spam label and never making it to our inboxes.

"None of my real e-mails have slipped into the spam folder and I remember only one spam reaching my inbox in the period I've been using Gmail. Spam is the bane of the Internet and it is refreshing to see Gmail put up such a good fight against it."—Eric, who wrote into our support team. (Jackson, 2007, n.p.)

As teachers, we don't want to spend countless hours poring over junk mail and deleting from our inboxes. We don't want students to encounter "adult" content in e-mail or phishing scams either. With Gmail's advanced filtering services, this is no longer a concern.

Google Chat

This is a big advantage to using Gmail over a traditional e-mail client. Gmail has the ability to enable two or more users to live chat with one another. Imagine, rather than running down the hall to ask a colleague a question, you can simply type the query and get an immediate response. The old method involved sending a message that went into someone's inbox, to be retrieved some time down the line. Chat puts you in touch with a contact right when you need the person. Located along the left side of the Gmail page, you'll find it's easy to use and a great way to communicate.

Google Chat in Gmail is a good tool for students to use while working on group projects. In Google Chat, multiple students can communicate with one another at the same time. As we've mentioned, collaboration shouldn't be limited to a particular location, and having access to live chat is an effective way to have students share ideas with one another.

■ SETTING UP GOOGLE CHAT

To set up the Google Chat function, take the following steps (see Figure 3.4):

1. You'll want to add your colleagues to your list of contacts. That way, when they are available for chat (i.e., when they are at their computer

using Gmail or iGoogle and you see they have a green light next to their name), you can jump right into a live conversation.

2. To add a contact, you'll need your colleague's Gmail address. With the address in hand, go into the chat search box and enter the address.

3. You'll be prompted to send the person either an e-mail or an invite to chat. Once a chat invite has been sent and accepted, that contact will now be part of your chat list in the future.

Figure 3.4 Setting Up Google Chat

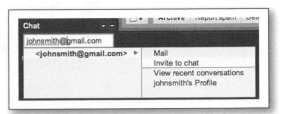

Project Idea: Using GmailVideo With a Guest Presenter

One of the coolest classroom innovations is the ability to video chat right in Gmail (Simple K12, 2010). While there are other programs that can facilitate this happening (e.g., Skype), probably the biggest advantage with Gmail is that because it is so widely used, it's easy to access video chat without having to create a new account. When you're trying to get a guest lecturer for your classroom, the easier you can make things, the better. Imagine bringing an author, athlete, politician, or entertainer into the walls of your classroom to talk with your students. Our "schools will go from 'buildings' to 'nerve centers,' with walls that are porous and transparent, connecting teachers, students and the community to the wealth of knowledge that exists in the world" (21st Century Schools, 2010).

Setting up the chat is easy, but let's be sure to cover how this is done (see Figure 3.5).

> **NETS-S Standard 2 Objective a**
>
> Students use digital media and environments to communicate and work collaboratively, including at a distance, to support individual learning and contribute to the learning of others. Students interact, collaborate, and publish with peers, experts, or others employing a variety of digital environments and media. (ISTE, 2007)

- The first items you'll need to make a video chat work are a microphone and a webcam. Depending on the computer you're using, these may already be part of the internal tools (i.e., if you have a Mac computer, you're set!). If you don't have a mic and a webcam, they're fairly inexpensive to purchase and well worth the money.
- The most important step to enabling video chat within Gmail is acquiring a simple "plug-in" from Google.
  - To download the plug-in, click on the drop-down menu in the Chat area along the left side of the Gmail screen.
  - You'll find a menu for Chat Settings. Look in the area for Voice and Video Chat. You'll find a link that will help you access the plug-in.
  - Alternatively, you could use the following link to download the tool: http://google-voice-and-video.en.softonic.com/

- Once the plug-in is installed on the computer, you'll find that you now have a green video camera icon next to your name in the Chat window. This means you can now launch audio and video chats in addition to normal text chats.

- Any of your contacts that have enabled video chat on their computers will have the video camera icon next to their names as well.
- Now that the plug-in is up and running, the only remaining settings for video chat involve enabling a camera, mic, and speakers. Once they're all hooked up to the computer, you're ready to go!

Figure 3.5 Setting Up Video Chat in Gmail

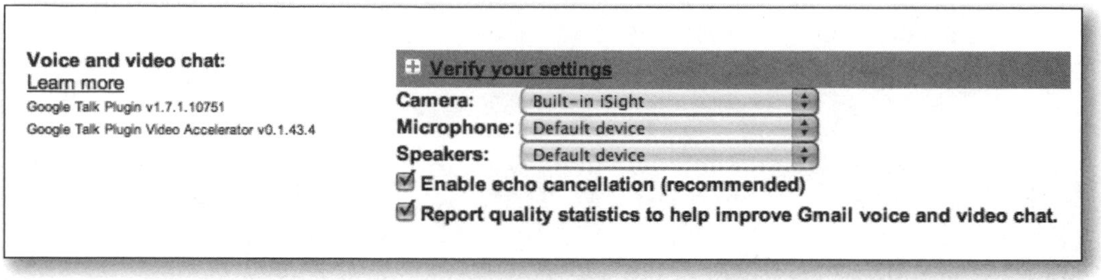

Voice and video chat:
Learn more
Google Talk Plugin v1.7.1.10751
Google Talk Plugin Video Accelerator v0.1.43.4

⊞ **Verify your settings**
Camera: Built-in iSight
Microphone: Default device
Speakers: Default device
☑ Enable echo cancellation (recommended)
☑ Report quality statistics to help improve Gmail voice and video chat.

Here are a couple of pieces of advice when it comes to microphones:

1. Buy a microphone that has a USB connection. The mini-plug type may be cheaper, but they don't work on every machine and it's easy to overlook the connection as the problem.
2. If you're broadcasting the audio from your guest speaker to the entire classroom, you'll want a mic that isn't part of a headset combo. It's easy to find a stand-alone microphone, and they generally work well.

MORE IDEAS FOR GOING GOOGLE

Other Good Gmail Options for Schools

- Students can have fun doing the morning announcements using video chat in Gmail. They can use the program to conduct interviews with other students or various members of the community.
- Parent–Teacher Conferences may be changed forever in the future. Can you imagine having a one-on-one with a parent from your computer screen? You can quickly look up information and share it with parents, without leaving your classroom. Conducting meetings like this could be very valuable for reaching those living in rural areas.

TIPS FOR THE GOOGLE CLASSROOM

- If you're already using a different e-mail client at school, try using Gmail for a while as a personal e-mail account. It gives will give you the chance to test some of the features we've discussed while providing you with options to retain both accounts.
- Tired of having multiple e-mail accounts to check daily? Gmail can receive the e-mails from other clients. Here are some instructions from Google for how to make this happen: http://gmailblog.blogspot.com/2009/05/import-your-mail-and-contacts-from .html. It takes a few minutes to set up the Gmail system, but once it is in place, you can check all your e-mail from one location.

4

Google Sites

FIVE THINGS TO KNOW ABOUT GOOGLE SITES

1. You can create multiple sites, but there is a size limit of 1 GB for your account.
2. Templates can help make your site creation easier.
3. You can use a variety of files on your site including images, docs, videos, and more.
4. Sites can be public or private.
5. Student projects can include a work portfolio or a WebQuest.

TWENTY-FIRST CENTURY LEARNING ■

Use communication for a range of purposes [e.g., to inform, instruct, motivate and persuade].

—Partnership for 21st Century Skills, 2004

Creating a classroom website is an important way to communicate and share with your key stakeholders: parents and students. Using Google Sites, you can not only create your own classroom site, but students can also create a web presence to share some of their ideas and projects.

In this chapter, we'll look at how you can create your classroom website using Google Sites. We'll also discover how you can help students build an online portfolio of their work. Finally, we'll explore a classroom project called a WebQuest that has students conduct research in an online activity that encourages higher-level thinking.

Project Idea: Building a Classroom Website Using a Template

Getting started with Google Sites is simple. Rather than starting your own Google site from scratch, let's look at creating a classroom website using a school-formatted template from Google. Here are the steps to take:

1. Go to sites.google.com.

2. Select **Create Site.**

3. Choose the **Classroom Template.**

4. Provide your site name. It must be a unique name.

5. Type in the word verification security code.

6. Click **Create Site.**

You've now got a default template on your Google site. Now let's customize the site for your information.

The site you've created is specifically formatted for a teacher. As you've probably noticed, though, it is already populated with generic classroom content. You'll need to go through and customize the pages with your announcements, assignments, a calendar, and more. As you edit the different pages in the site, be sure to think about what pages you'd like to keep and which ones you'd like to change or remove. For example, you may not want to have an Extra Credit page on your site, but you will want to keep the Calendar page.

■ ADDING, EDITING, AND DELETING PAGES

The Classroom Template comes with certain links and pages already intact, but there may be a page or two you'd like to create for your classroom website. Perhaps you'd like a page to display your grading policy, or you'd like to have a page of student work for display.

In addition, you will certainly want to edit the pages with Latin instead of English text. The calendar page will also need to be edited so you can include your classroom calendar instead of generic filler.

Finally, there are bound to be pages that don't fit with your classroom structure. These pages will need to be deleted from the site.

Adding New Pages

+ Create page

1. Click on the **Create Page** button. It's located in the top right corner of the screen.

Figure 4.1 Choose a Page Template

2. Select the appropriate **template** for your new page (see Figure 4.1). There are four types of page templates for you to choose from: Web Page, Announcements, File Cabinet, or List.

   a. Web Page: This is the basic style of page. You can insert any type of content you'd like on this page.

   b. Announcements: This is the blog style page in Google Sites. Content is added in posts and appears chronologically on the page.

   c. File Cabinet: This page is used for file storage in Google Sites. You can add a variety of file types including PDF, images, Word files, etc.

   d. List: If you want to create a list of items, this is your page. Perhaps you want a weekly spelling list, or a page for vocabulary.

3. **Name** your new page.

4. Choose whether to have your new page on the **top level** of your site, or if it will be a subordinate page.

5. Click **Create Page.**

Editing Your Pages

- Click on the **Edit Page** button. It's located in the top right corner of the screen.

- As you first get started, you'll want to click on the **Tips** at the top of each page. This will give you a step-by-step list, helping you adjust the current page.

Figure 4.2 Removing an Element From a Page

- Different sections of the page are editable: You can delete the sections and create your own content or change the current content.

- To change the name of a page, click on the current name and edit the text. Doing this will change the link name along the left side of the screen.

- To remove an existing content element from the page, click on the object (see Figure 4.2). The properties bar will display along the bottom of the element. Click **Remove** from the properties, and it will delete the content.

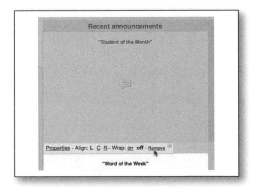

- To add new content to the site, click on the **Insert** menu. Located in the top left corner of the screen, you'll find various options for content elements you can add to your site.

Deleting a Page

- Click on the **More Actions** button. It's located along the top right side of the screen.
- Choose **Delete Page.** Even though the page is no longer present, there will still be a link in the sidebar navigation. We'll need to delete that at some point.

■ ADDING CONTENT TO YOUR SITE

Figure 4.3 Insert Menu Options

Using the **Insert** menu, there are several different elements you can add to your Google site (see Figure 4.3). It's important to consider some of the key information parents and students will want from your classroom site. Parents and students want to know due dates for assignments in a calendar. They want information about projects from online documents. Let's look at adding some of the elements found under the Insert menu.

Adding the Calendar

A calendar is an essential element that should be part of every classroom website. Parents and students are extremely interested in understanding when assignments are due and when classroom activities will occur. Because the calendar is a Google tool, it integrates seamlessly into Google Sites.

To add a Google Calendar,

1. Select **Calendar** from the **Insert** menu. You'll see the list of your Google Calendars.

2. Pick the calendar you'd like to add, and the **settings** window will appear.

3. Choose from the different options (size, color, etc.), and your calendar will show up on your page.

Once the calendar is on your website, any additions or edits you make in Google Calendar will appear in Google Sites.

Adding Photos From Picasa

1. Select **Picasa Photo** from the **Insert** menu.

2. Choose an image from one of your Picasa Web Albums.

The photo will display on your page. You can then adjust the size of the image.

Adding a Picasa Web Slideshow

Photos and slideshows are terrific elements to add to your site. Photos of students and classroom activities provide a wonderful way for teachers to build community between school and home. Parents will be excited that they can see their student engaged in the classroom, and students will feel good that they are getting acknowledgment for their work at school.

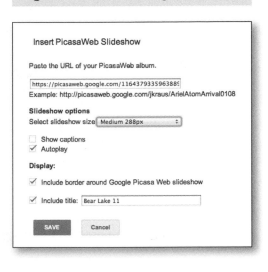

Figure 4.4 Embedding a Slideshow

1. Select Picasa Web slideshow from the Insert menu (see Figure 4.4).

2. You'll be prompted to use images from your Google+ Photo Albums.

3. Select the album you want from the visual menu.

4. Choose your desired options for the slideshow including size, captions, and auto play.

5. Decide on your preferred display options. This includes adding a border and a title.

6. Click **Save.**

Adding Video

Video can serve a few different purposes for your classroom website. You can share videos from classroom activities with parents and students. These can include student presentations in class, club activities, field trips, and more.

Video can be used as an instructional tool. Whether it's making your own videos to help students with concepts and assignments, or finding videos online to help students understand your curriculum, video can dramatically enhance your students' ability to grasp concepts.

Another effective method of sharing video on your website is as a student showcase. When students create videos for their projects in class, Google Sites allows them to easily promote those videos.

1. Select **Video** from the **Insert** menu (see Figure 4.5).

Figure 4.5 Inserting Video

2. Choose among using YouTube, Google Video, or Google Docs Videos to display your movie.

3. To insert a video, you'll need to know its URL (videos in your Google Docs will automatically display if you select that choice). Go to either Google Video or YouTube and search

for your video. You'll find the URL beneath the video using the **Share** button. Copy this URL.

4. Paste the URL in the **Open** field in the dialog window.

5. Choose from other video options including adding a border or a title.

One of the best ways to utilize Google Docs as part of your website is to embed forms on your Google site. The form is easy to find, and the results are sent to you immediately.

■ ADDING DOCS, SPREADSHEETS, PRESENTATIONS, AND FORMS

Figure 4.6 Adding a Form

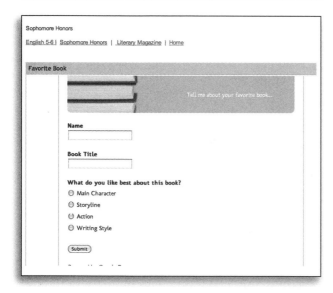

As part of your instruction, you utilize a variety of files to help students with the curriculum. You make handouts, teach using multimedia presentations, compile data to make analysis, and gather information from students. We've already looked at Google Docs as a way to make these different types of files. Now Google Sites can be used to display the files on your website.

Adding Forms

To add a form to your site, do the following (see Figure 4.6):

1. Select **Documents, Spreadsheets,** or **Spreadsheet Form** from the Insert menu.

2. A list of your Google Docs or Spreadsheets will appear in the window. Choose the file you'd like to display on your Google site. The spreadsheet will have one additional display option, as you can choose between a published spreadsheet and an editable spreadsheet.

3. Once you pick the desired file, you'll have several display options to choose from including title of the document or spreadsheet, a border for the file, and the display size of the file in *pixels.*

4. Align your file on the Google site using the **options** bar. After setting up the way your file looks on the page, the **properties** bar helps you determine how other elements on the page will interact with the file.

5. Click Save to preview your file. Use the Edit page button and select the object to change.

Adding Presentations

To add a presentation, do the following (see Figure 4.7):

1. Select **Presentations** from the **Insert** menu.

2. A list of your presentations will display in the window. Choose your selected presentation.

3. As with the other Google Docs tools, you'll be able to create boarders or use titles with your presentation. Unique to presentations is the ability to auto start the presentation or to have the slideshow loop once completed.

Adding presentation from Google Docs is a great way to share content from your class with parents and students. Those students who were absent from class can follow along with materials from home. Students looking to review a concept learned earlier can recap information at their own pace.

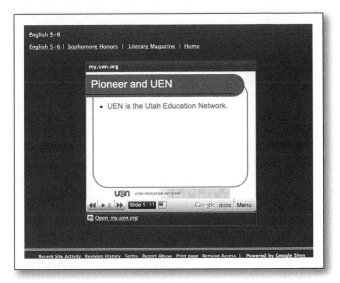

Figure 4.7 Adding a Presentation

NAVIGATION FOR YOUR SITE ■

As you customize your classroom website from the premade template, you'll find there are several links to pages going down the left side of the screen. While there are some great ideas for possible pages for your classroom site, you should adapt the links to the pages you want on your site.

A classroom website should be easy to navigate and straightforward regarding content. Parents want quick access to the most important information, which includes due dates, project requirements, contact information, and classroom resources. The template we used to set up a classroom website has several of these pages. The template includes three separate submenus of links to pages.

The first set of links includes the Homepage for the site, Homework Assignments, Extra Credit, and Contact Me. Remember, earlier we saw how you can delete unwanted pages. The problem was that the link still remained in the sidebar. You can remove any of these links to deleted pages (see Figure 4.8).

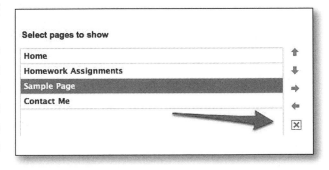

Figure 4.8 Deleting an Existing Link in a Sidebar

To Remove a Link in the Sidebar

1. Select **Edit Sidebar.** This is located at the bottom of the sidebar.

2. You're now on the **Site Layout** page. Click on the **edit** button below the first Navigation area.

3. A page will display showing the links in this section of the sidebar. Select the page you'd like to remove, and click on the **X** button in the lower right corner of the menu.

You have successfully removed that link from the sidebar.

To Add a Link in the Sidebar

By creating a new page in your website, you'll be prompted to include a link to the page in your sidebar navigation.

1. Choose the **Put Page at the top level** option when creating the page, and the link will be automatically added.

2. You can add a link to an external site using the **Add URL** link.

To Edit a Link in the Sidebar

You can't change an existing link in the sidebar. You'll need to just delete the unwanted link and create a new one.

Adding or Editing Content in the Sidebar

Not only can you have a navigation menu going down the sidebar of your page, but you can also add or edit other types of content in this area (see Figure 4.9). Since we're using the Classroom Template, let's explore how to edit the existing sidebar content.

Figure 4.9   Editing Elements in the Sidebar

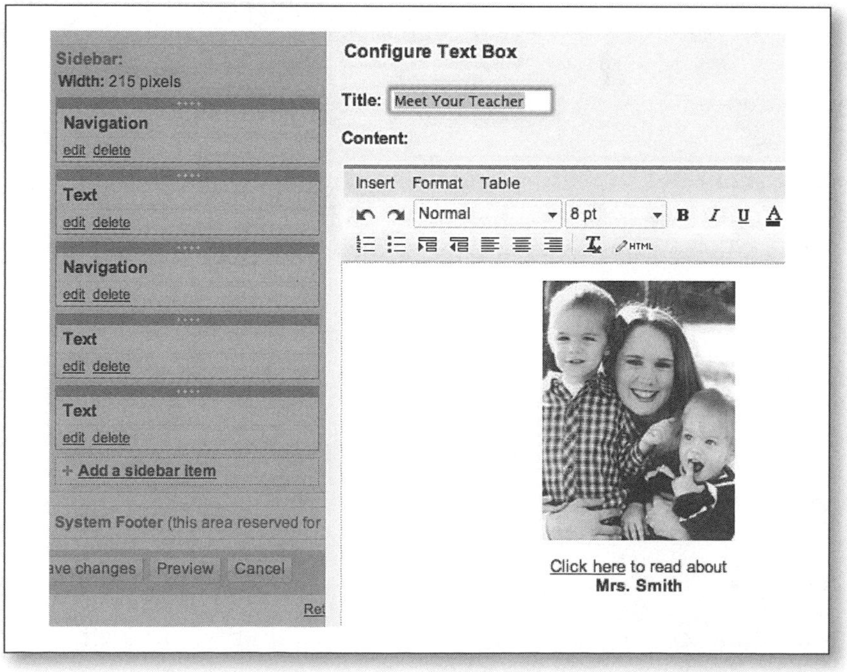

Click **Edit Sidebar.** You'll find several different elements in the sidebar that you can edit. Each field is named based upon its content style. Click **Edit** in the left corner of the element you wish to change. The element will open, and you can edit the content inside.

For example, let's change the image and link in the Meet Your Teacher text element.

1. Click on the top text field. This will launch the edit mode for this field. You can change the text by typing your own content.

2. To change the image, click on the existing image and use the **remove** link.

3. To insert your own image, click on the **Insert** menu and select **image.**

4. Either upload an image, or use an image from the Internet as your profile picture.

5. The link that goes to the About Me page doesn't need to be changed. You'll just need to open that page and update the information with your own bio and images.

6. Click **Done** when finished.

Adding new content to the sidebar can provide your users with the information they're interested in. Here's how to create a new field in the sidebar:

1. Click Add a sidebar item.

+ Add a sidebar item

2. A window will open giving you a variety of new page elements to choose from. You can add a link through the **Navigation** element, text and images using the **Text** element, or site information using either the **Activity** elements or the **Site** elements.

3. Add your desired elements. They will appear in the list along the sidebar.

4. Click the Save Changes button when you're done.

Don't forget, this template has different tutorials to help you make certain customizations. The **Template tips** are found in the lower left corner of your site. These types of tips are found throughout this template, and they can really help you work with the various pages. Check them out!

CUSTOMIZING THE LOOK ■
AND FEEL OF YOUR SITE

One of the best things about Google Sites is the ability to adapt the way the site looks to your individual taste. Since we've used a template, much of the design was previously customized. Still, there are several changes we can make to customize the site. Let's change the site's general appearance (see Figure 4.10).

1. Click on the **More Actions** button to get started.

2. Select the **Manage Site** option.

Figure 4.10 Changing the Site's Appearance

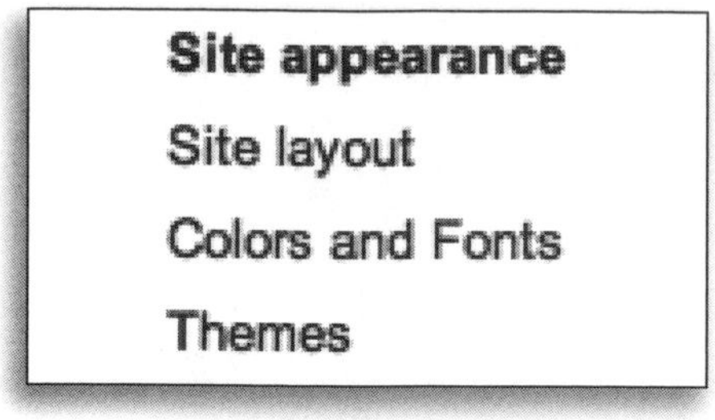

Site appearance

Site layout

Colors and Fonts

Themes

Figure 4.11 Change Your Header Logo

Configure site logo

Select Logo:
⊙ Custom Logo

uen
UTAH EDUCATION NETWORK

Attach a file: (Choose File)

3. To change the appearance of the site, go to the Site Appearance area in the lower left corner of the screen. Here you can choose from Site Layout, Colors and Fonts, and Themes as options to edit the look and feel of your site. Under the Site Layout option, you can change the Header, Footer, and Sidebar of your website. We've already discussed changing the sidebar, but a great way to customize your site is to change the header logo (see below and Figure 4.11).

Changing the Header Logo

1. Under the Header field, click on **Change Logo.**

2. You will be prompted to add your own custom logo by attaching a file. You can add any image as a header, but the typical header is small and usually fits in the upper left corner of a site.

Colors and Fonts

You have the option to change everything about the page, from Background Color, to Link colors, to fonts themselves. You even have a Preview window to see your potential changes.

Themes

When we started this teacher website, we used the Classroom Template. If you want to use something else, however, there are a variety of themes to choose from in the Sites Gallery. There are two major options for changing the theme of your site.

1. Choose from the basic **Sites Gallery.** There are about 30 different themes that can replace the Classroom Template. Select the theme you'd like and click **Apply.**

2. Browse the **Templates Gallery.** There is a collection of templates for schools and education. Once you find the template you like, you can apply it to your site.

■ USING YOUR CLASSROOM WEBSITE

Once you have your Google site together, there are a few things to consider to make your site an effective tool.

Updating the Content

It is so important to keep the content on your site current. No parent or student will value a site that is woefully out-of-date. Make sure the calendar has current events being displayed. Homework should reflect the projects the students are currently working on. Google Sites makes it easy to replace old content with new, but it requires having a plan to make the necessary changes.

Providing Relevant Content

The information on your website should help students accomplish assignments and learn more about the materials they are studying in class. Be sure you share any handouts or training materials you used in class. Other important documents for your website may include a syllabus, disclosure statement, grading policy, fieldtrip permission slips, and any additional forms for class. It's also useful to include links to sites where students can get additional information about the content from your curriculum.

Marketing Your Site

I'm not suggesting you need to place an ad on the web or in the local paper, but you should have an idea of how you'll let parents and students know about your website. First, be sure your site is linked to your school's website. This is the first place parents will look for you online. Next, let parents and students know you keep the site up-to-date and that you'll be using the site to share helpful information with them. Give them the address to your site at Back-to-School Night or at a Parent–Teacher Conference. Add the URL for your site to your disclosure statement or syllabus you give to students during the first week of school.

Project Idea: Creating a WebQuest

Creating a WebQuest using Google Sites is an excellent way to have students conduct research online using a structured, self-paced method. Often, when students are asked to perform a research activity online, it falls into one of two camps: an Internet-based scavenger hunt, or a loosely organized Google search where anything goes. A WebQuest looks to provide students with high-quality web resources that offer content-based information in an organized, online activity.

What Is a WebQuest?

A WebQuest is an inquiry-oriented lesson format in which most or all the information that learners work with comes from the web. The model was developed by Bernie Dodge at San Diego State University in February 1995, and since its inception, tens of thousands of teachers have embraced WebQuests as a way

NETS T Standard 2 Objective a

Teachers design, develop, and evaluate authentic learning experiences and assessment incorporating contemporary tools and resources to maximize content learning in context and to develop the knowledge, skills, and attitudes identified in the NETS•S. Teachers design or adapt relevant learning experiences that incorporate digital tools and resources to promote student learning and creativity. (ISTE, 2008)

to make good use of the Internet while engaging their students in the kinds of thinking that the 21st century requires (Dodge, 2007).

A WebQuest consists of five major components that are developed in an online environment. These elements include the Introduction, Task, Process, Evaluation, and Conclusion. All of these parts work together to provide students with a rich online experience. Let's take a closer look at the basic elements of a WebQuest. You'll also find a lot of great WebQuest information at http://teacherworld.com/webquest.html and www.internet 4classrooms.com/using_quest.htm.

Introduction

In a short paragraph, you'll want to do the following:

- Introduce students to the WebQuest.
- Set the stage or provide background for the upcoming activity.
- Motivate students and capture their interest. Think about creating an educational "hook" for your activity.

Task

Next, write a short paragraph or outline of expected results.

- The task is the end result of student efforts, not the steps involved in getting there.
- This section helps focus the learner and clearly describes the essential questions and student learning objective.
- It is important to engage students in an "authentic task," something that has meaning beyond the classroom.

Process

The process section lays out the entire activity. Be sure to provide enough information that students can work independently.

- Describe how the groups will be assigned and the role of each member.
- List the steps that the students will need to follow in order to complete the activity.
- List any materials and resources that the students will need for the activity. In particular, you will need to list websites in this section.

Evaluation

Traditional forms of assessment usually don't fit into the WebQuest model. One popular form of assessment is a rubric for evaluating WebQuests.

- Provide students with the evaluation criteria.
- Make students aware of their responsibilities with the WebQuest.

Conclusion

Encourage the students to form their own conclusions from what they learned as a result of the WebQuest.

- Provide students with additional information, activities, or links that will enable them to explore information beyond this WebQuest.
- Give students the chance to reflect upon the activities and what they've learned.

Why Use WebQuests?

Developing a WebQuest is a fairly involved process that will require the teacher to prepare a lot of information and find a variety of online resources. So, why would a teacher want to put the time into developing a WebQuest? Here are some key ideas on the rationale behind this effective teaching tool from Tom March, one of the leading innovators of WebQuests.

Student Motivation and Authenticity—When students are motivated, they not only put in more effort, but their minds are more alert and ready to make connections.

Developing Thinking Skills—One of the main ... features of any WebQuest is that students tackle questions that prompt higher-level thinking.

Cooperative Learning—. . . [I]n WebQuests, students take on roles within a small student group and this tends to promote motivation.

Process and Access—Research has shown that the most important factor related to student learning and technology use is how teachers relate the technology-based activity to other learning activities. (Teacher Created Materials, 2002, n.p.)

DEVELOPING A WEBQUEST ■
USING GOOGLE SITES

We've seen how a WebQuest can be an effective teaching and learning tool for your classroom. Google Sites is a great way to build and share your WebQuest with students. Here are some of the basic steps for creating your WebQuest and some ideas for using Google Sites in its development.

1. Go to sites.google.com.

2. Click **Create New Site.**

3. Choose **Browse the gallery** for more options.

4. Type WebQuest in the search box.

5. The first template is the WebQuest Template from Patricia McGee. Select **Preview Template.**

Figure 4.12 Choose the WebQuest Template

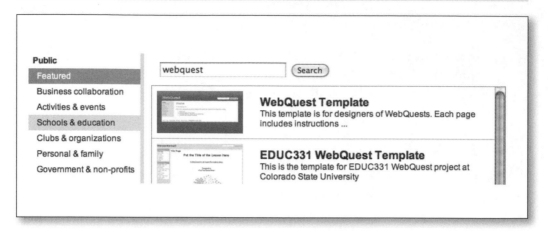

6. By previewing the WebQuest template, you'll find the site already includes the five main elements you need for your WebQuest. Each of the pages includes details concerning the steps of the WebQuest and provides you with ideas for developing the page. Apply the template with the **Use this Template** button located in the top right of your screen (see Figure 4.12).

7. You'll be prompted to name and establish the settings for the WebQuest. This follows the same procedure you've done before with other Google sites.

8. Your WebQuest structure is now set. You'll need to update the pages with the appropriate content. Remember, each page has suggestions of possible content and formatting ideas. There are also links to existing WebQuests to give you examples.

9. Customize your pages by deleting the current content and add the content for your subject. Remember you can add images, links, documents, videos, and so forth to help provide activities and resources for your WebQuest.

Project Idea: Creating a Digital Student Portfolio

A student portfolio isn't a new concept. Many of you have been tracking student writing and assignments in folders that have been stored in the classroom. Portfolios are a great way to help students organize their materials, as the content is all located in one place.

The problem is that the traditional portfolio has become fairly antiquated. It only allows for a paper-based project and doesn't account for the wide array of digital assignments currently being created. While it's still a useful way to track student writing, the portfolio has needed an update to meet the needs of 21st century learners.

The electronic portfolio has evolved as an effective method for storing and sharing students' digital projects. A website is a terrific venue for this content, as it can be updated and shared with parents, peers, and teachers.

What Is a Student Portfolio?

A student portfolio is a collection of student works over a period of time. A portfolio generally is seen as a performance-based assessment tool. It is used for evaluation, as it demonstrates how and what the student is learning. An electronic portfolio simply means that the portfolio is digitally created and shared.

> A portfolio is the story of knowing. Knowing about things. . . . Knowing oneself . . . Knowing an audience . . . Portfolios are students' own stories of what they know, why they believe they know it, and why others should be of the same opinion. A portfolio is opinion backed by fact . . . Students prove what they know with samples of their work. (Paulson, Paulson, & Meyer, 1991, p. 60)

What Are the Key Elements of a Student Portfolio?

Portfolios can come in several different media types. The projects can reflect a wide array of standards. But there are a few things that are common among portfolios, regardless of their purpose and format. Student portfolios should include the following elements:

- Learner Objectives: These objectives can come from state and national standards. You should have students clearly identify what skill(s) they are looking to illustrate with an artifact in the portfolio.
- Guidelines for Selecting Materials: Working with the teacher, students should choose projects that reflect their best work. "The portfolio is a laboratory where students construct meaning from their accumulated experience" (Paulson et al., 1991, p. 61).
- Artifacts: These consist of student projects that demonstrate the learning objectives. As part of a Google-enhanced classroom, many of these projects should be stored in Google Docs, Picasa, or other Google tools. Working collaboratively, the teacher and student will determine the appropriate number of artifacts for the portfolio.
- Self-Reflection: One of the most important elements of a student portfolio is reflection. As students choose artifacts for their Google site, they should reflect upon how the project is an accurate depiction of their content knowledge. Reflection can come in the form of a blog post, or it can be shared as a simple text box.

NETS S Standard 3 Objective c

Students apply digital tools to gather, evaluate, and use information. Students evaluate and select information sources and digital tools based on the appropriateness to specific tasks. (ISTE, 2007)

- Teacher Feedback: Assessment from the teacher is a key difference between a student portfolio and a student website. Once the student has identified curriculum standards and demonstrated his or her understanding of those learning objective through artifacts and reflection, the teacher provides important insights into the success of those academic measures. In many ways, teacher feedback validates the effectiveness of the student portfolio.

Five Key Stages to Creating an Online Portfolio

Stage 1:   Setting Up the Definitions of Your Portfolio

Be sure to identify the Purpose of your portfolio, select the Standards of your portfolio, and recognize the Audience for your portfolio.

Stage 2:   Developing Your Portfolio

Create the Google Site for the portfolio. This should include creating the various pages you intend to use as part of the site.

Collect the educational artifacts for the portfolio. Students should identify which projects they intend to include in their portfolio.

Stage 3:   Student Reflection

Students should write reflective statements about each artifact and why it was included in the portfolio.

Students should set goals for improvement on educational skills.

Stage 4:   Adding the Artifacts

Artifacts should demonstrate the student's understanding and application of the desired standard.

It's good to have students use a variety of projects, which reflect different types of media and literacies.

Google Sites is an effective tool for adding artifacts as the site can incorporate files from documents to videos.

Stage 5:   Presenting the Portfolio

Students will share their portfolio with the appropriate audience. This is typically the teacher, but it may include a potential employer or recruiter (adapted from http://sites.google.com/site/eportfolio apps/overview/process).

Building a Student Portfolio Using Google Sites

Using Google's tools makes creating a student portfolio much easier, as many of the artifacts you will want included are stored in Google Docs, Picasa Web Album, or other Google products. Since the tools work hand-in-hand with one another, you can insert these files into your Google site seamlessly.

Rather than using a premade template for the student portfolio for this project, we'll be building our Google site from scratch. Let's get started.

1. Go to sites.google.com.

2. Click **Create New Site.**

3. Select the **Blank Template.**

4. Select a **Theme** for your site. There are several to choose from, and you can always update this later.

5. Under More Options, you can add a **description** of your site. You can also choose whether to make your site **available to everyone in the world** or only to **people you specify.**

6. Provide the name of the site, and enter the appropriate security code.

7. Click **Create Site.**

Since this is a blank site, you'll need to create all the pages for your student portfolio. Remember that you'll want to use the different page templates to create the right style of page for the intended content. For example, you'll want your students to use the announcements style of page for their personal reflections.

Creating the Pages

To get started with our new portfolio site, let's make the pages we'll need to display our content. Pages are all created in the same manner; only the template you use will differ. Here is the basic outline for creating your pages:

1. Click **Create Page.**

2. Choose the **template.**

3. **Name** the page.

4. Choose the **Put the page at the top level** option.

5. Click **Create Page.** The page will appear on the screen, and a link to the page should display in the sidebar.

Possible pages for the site include Introduction, Reflection, Artifacts, Learner Objectives, and Teacher Feedback. Let's look at some content options for these pages.

Introduction: Students should use the standard **Web** template option when creating this page. This page should contain an overview paragraph that states the general purpose for the portfolio. Other possible elements for this page include the following:

- Image—Use either a picture of the student or some picture that deals with the content of the portfolio (i.e., for a writing portfolio, you could use a picture of a pencil and paper).
- Table of Contents—Share which pages are part of the portfolio and a sentence about each one's content.
- Contact Information—If students plan to use the portfolio as part of a job search, contact information is a must.

Reflection: The template for this page is the **Announcements** option. To use this page, your students will be blogging. Rather than writing in text boxes, blogs utilize posts. These posts will be organized chronologically on the page, with newer entries at the top and older content further down the page. Here's how to blog in Google Sites.

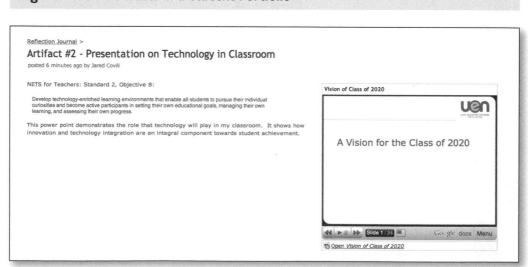

1. Click **New Post** to create your first entry.

2. Provide a **Title** for your entry by replacing the Untitled Post text in the appropriate box.

3. Use the provided text box to compose your thoughts. There are editing controls along the top of the page. The editing tools give you options from formatting text to adding content to the layout and more.

4. You can use the reflection page as a way to display portfolio artifacts and reflect upon them on the same page. Use the **Insert** menu to add artifacts using different Google tools as part of your site. Remember, you can insert images, Google Docs, YouTube videos, and more into a post on your blog.

5. When you complete a post, click **Save.**

Objectives and Learner Standards: Students can use the Web template to create these pages. The basic elements for these pages include national and state standards embodied by the artifacts in the portfolio. A great place to find these standards may include the NETS (National Educational Technology Standards), ISTE or a variety of national and state curriculum standards.

Artifacts: One option for the artifacts page is to use the **File Cabinet** template. With this template, you can upload a variety of files for evaluation. The size limit is 12 MB per file, so you can include documents, PowerPoints, spreadsheets, images, and more (see Figure 4.13).

Figure 4.13 Artifacts in a Student Portfolio

To add files to the artifacts page,

1. Select the **Add File** button.

2. A window will appear, prompting you to browse your computer for the file or to provide the URL for a file.

3. Choose the text to display. If none is provided, the file name will display.

4. Provide a file description. This is a good place to reflect upon the artifact or to share a brief summary of the file.

5. Click the **Upload** button.

Teacher Feedback: The final page in the student portfolio is for teacher feedback. To create this page, let's use the **Announcements** template. In order for the teacher to provide feedback, he or she needs to first be added to the site as a collaborator.

To add a collaborator to your site,

1. Select the **More** button in the top right corner of the screen.

2. Choose **Site Permissions** from the list of settings. It should be the last item (see Figure 4.14).

3. Enter in the e-mail address of the collaborator.

4. Select the level of permission you'd like to give the new collaborator. To make someone an editor, he or she will need to have the option **To Edit** chosen.

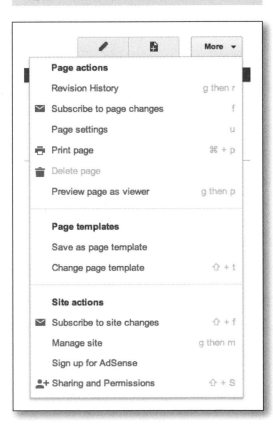

Figure 4.14 Settings in Google Sites

5. Hit the **Share** button, thus sending the person an e-mail invitation to collaborate on the site. This gives the teacher the ability to add comments and provide feedback for the portfolio.

Once you've created all the pages for your site, it's time to add all the content to the pages. We've already discussed possible content for the various pages. Google Sites makes it easy to add and edit all of your desired content.

Sharing the Completed Portfolio

So, the students have created their portfolios, and now it's time to share them with the appropriate audience. There are three permission levels that allow students to share their portfolios (see Figure 4.15):

1. **Public on the web**—The site is searchable and viewable to anyone online.

Figure 4.15   Sharing Settings in Google Sites

2. **Anyone with the link**—If you share the link to your site, anyone who uses the link will have access to the site. Both this option and the one above are open to the public, as they do not require a sign-in to view the portfolio.

3. **Private**—Only a site administrator can provide access to this site. Users must sign in to the site, and their e-mail address must be preapproved. This is the most secure form of access to the student portfolio, and it the preferred one for many teachers.

One of the best things about sharing an electronic student portfolio is that it can be updated from year to year. Once the structure is in place, content can be added and removed. Reflections can be updated to show student growth. Evaluation can take place over a student's career, instead of merely focusing on a particular assignment or grade level.

MORE IDEAS FOR GOING GOOGLE

More Possible Google Sites

- Create a site for your school club or sports team: Google Sites can help you share announcements or calendar items about upcoming events for your group. Parents can see photos from recent activities. As the teacher, you can provide access to different materials that are important for your students.
- Create a student *wiki* for a research project: Because Google Sites has the ability to add collaborators, you can have student work on a wiki in groups. Each of the students can add his or her own content to the site and develop a really interesting research wiki.

TIPS FOR THE GOOGLE CLASSROOM

- Before students start creating their site with Google Sites, have them create an outline of the content they would like to add to their projects. It really helps to have an idea of what pages you'll need to create for your site and what material you plan to put on each page.
- Be sure the students add you, as the teacher, as a collaborator on their sites. Often, students will forget to give you access, and then they'll make the site private. Make sure you can add comments and suggestions to the students' Google sites.
- You have up to 100 MB of space per site. This provides you with ample room for data storage, but you won't be able to load tons of multimedia files to your Google site. Be sure to take advantage of additional Google tools (i.e., Docs, Picasa, and YouTube) to house a lot of your larger multimedia files. Remember, you can always insert a copy of the files into your Google site from the other Google resources.

5

Blogger

FIVE THINGS TO KNOW ABOUT BLOGGER

1. Creating a blog takes about 5 minutes.
2. Blogs post information chronologically, with newer information at the top.
3. Students can leave comments on blogs as a way to communicate with one another.
4. Blogs can contain multimedia content including images, video, presentations, and more.
5. Teachers can follow colleagues' blogs as part of their Personal Learning Network (**PLN**).

TWENTY-FIRST CENTURY LEARNING ■

Articulate thoughts and ideas effectively using oral, written and nonverbal communication skills in a variety of forms and contexts.

—Partnership for 21st Century Skills, 2004

Blogging has become an Internet phenomenon over the past decade. Blogger is Google's solution for teachers who want a website where they can share announcements without needing to understand anything about HTML or web creation.

Will Richardson, a noted educational blogger and author (2006), shared his thoughts on the impact of blogging and other web-based tools: "The biggest, most sweeping change in our relationship with the Internet may not be as much the ability to publish as it is the ability to share, connect, and create with many, many others of like minds and interests" (n.p.).

This vision is much different from the traditional classroom where most student work is done in isolation, never finding connections to a larger whole that might be produced by the class in its entirety. That's not to say that in this new world students don't do their own work. But it does mean that responsibility for that work is in some way shared. Learning is a continuous conversation among many participants.

Clarence Fished, a 7th- and 8th-grade Language Arts teacher from Canada, shared his thought on the importance of blogging for his students: "They're learning the technical skills, but they're also learning that they have a voice online," he said. "They may be from a tiny town in the middle of nowhere, but they're writing online, people are commenting on it, and they're learning that they have a voice" (quoted in Gilbert, 2005, n.p.).

What Is Blogging?

We've all heard about blogs for years, but what is a blog and what makes it unique?

At its core, a blog provides a space where people can share their thoughts and ideas with one another. Used in the school setting, it is an online journal where students can reflect and collaborate with their classmates. A traditional website generally consists of one-way communication; the teacher shares information about the classroom with parents and students. With a blog, the audience can also contribute by making comments.

Blogs are also different from traditional websites because they are subscribable. This means that parents and students can receive updates from your blog, and they can read your blog entries through a variety of online tools using an RSS feed. This makes your blog more available to your audience.

Why Should Students Blog in Schools?

We often hear of students sharing too much personal information online. Students can put comments on the Internet that have unintended consequences and that can cause them a variety of social problems with peers, family members, and school officials. So, why would we encourage them to blog as part of our curriculum? Here are a few reasons from David Warlick, author of www .twocentsworth.com and a leading voice on educational blogging:

Number 1: A blog is a Web-publishing concept that enables anyone— first graders, middle school teachers, high school principals, district superintendents—to publish information on the Internet.

Number 2: Blogs . . . or blogging has become a journalistic tool, a way to publish news, ideas, rants, announcements, and ponderings very quickly, and without technical, editorial, and time constraints. It essentially makes anyone a columnist. In fact, many established columnists now publish their own blogs.

Number 3: Blogs, because of their ease of use, and because of the context of news and editorial column writing, have become a highly effective way to help students to become better writers. Research has long shown that students write more, write in greater detail, and take greater care with spelling, grammar, and punctuation, when they are writing to an authentic audience over the Internet. (quoted in L. Jackson, 2011, n.p.)

As students blog, they open their thoughts up to their classmates as part of the public discourse. This helps students participate in a group forum where ideas are exchanged, opinions are discussed, and comments are provided. One of the key 21st century learning skills involves collaboration:

- Demonstrate ability to work effectively and respectfully with diverse teams (Partnership for 21st Century Learning, 2004, n.p.).

Blogging truly encourages students to respectfully share ideas with their peers. Even though an individual produces each post, the blog is an effective way to get feedback and communicate in a group process.

Why Should Teachers Blog?

Blogging has become a major tool in the 21st century teacher's bag of tricks. Because it is so easy to set up and maintain a blog, many teachers find it is an effective way to get their message out. Here are a few reasons teachers love to blog:

Communicate With Parents

A blog is a great way to communicate with parents. Unlike a traditional website, a blog provides a more personal way to share information. While a website is really good at providing the details about a classroom activity, a blog lets the teacher share the *effect* of that event on the students. Using images and video as part of the blog gives parents an intimate look into your classroom and helps build a strong sense of community.

Communicate With Colleagues

Teachers love to talk about education. Lots of educators blog so they can have a professional dialogue with their colleagues. As teachers share their ideas and advice on a variety of classroom issues, they can form a network of support for one another. Blogging also provides the teacher with a forum to share his or her ideas related to the classroom. More than just a "how to" on the act of teaching a lesson, blogging provides many teachers with a place to share their thoughts on the role of education.

Highlight Student Work

We've seen how many student projects are moving into the digital age. Not only are these assignments more engaging for the kids, but also electronic assignments can easily be showcased on a classroom blog. "Blogs can be used as a platform for highlighting the best work of your students, showcasing their talent to an audience that goes beyond the classroom" (Carvin, 2006, n.p.).

So, now that we've looked into the *why* of blogging, it's time to explore the *how* of creating your classroom blog. This section will detail how you go about making a blog, adding posts with multimedia content, and establishing the different settings you'll want for your blog.

■ CREATING A CLASSROOM BLOG

There are many different blogging tools available online (even with other Google tools like Google Sites), but we will be discussing Blogger because it is used so widely and is simple to manage. Once you have your Google account, setting up your blog is a breeze through Blogger. Let's get started.

Figure 5.1   Get Started Button

1. Go to www.blogger.com.

2. Select the **Get Started** button.

3. You'll be prompted to create a Google account to get started. Since you should already have an account created, there is a link near the top of the screen to sign in with your user name and password.

4. The next step is to **Create a new blog** (see Figure 5.2). There are a few elements to complete on this screen.

   a. **Blog Title:** This will appear at the top of your blog. It can be anything you'd like, but for a classroom blog, you'll probably want it to sound professional.

   b. **Blog Address:** This will be your blog's web address, or URL. You'll find that every Blogger blog has the same ending—blogspot.com—but you must provide a unique beginning for your address. This can be a little tricky, since there are millions of blogs in Blogger's database. You can always **Check the Availability** of your address with the provided link. Again, pick something you're willing to use with parents and students, as the address will be something you'll share with others.

   c. **Word Verification:** Blogger will require that you complete a word verification form to ensure that a real person, and not a computerized spammer, is creating a new blog.

   d. Pick a **starter template**: You can always change this later; in fact, after your blog gets created, there will be a lot more choices.

5. You've successfully created your blog with Blogger. Now it's time to add content and customize how your blog looks.

Figure 5.2   Creating Your Blog in Blogger

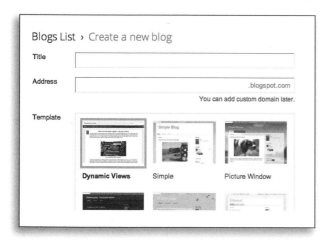

Writing and Editing Posts on Your Blog

With your blog created, you can begin sharing announcements, homework help, and other thoughts on your classroom with parents, students, and colleagues. Blogs are different from traditional websites in that they consist of individual bits of news and information called *posts.* As you write posts on your blog, older content moves down the page as newer content gets added.

Writing a Blog Post

1. To write your first entry on your new blog, click on the **Start Blogging** button (see Figure 5.3). If you've created a blog in the past and want to add a new post to it, you'll find a **New Post** button on your Dashboard in Blogger.

2. Blogger will load the New Post page, where you'll find a basic word processor.

3. Start your post by providing a **Title.** The title should relate to the content of your new post. For example, a title might be "Field Trip on Friday" if you're looking to make an announcement of the class's upcoming activity.

Figure 5.3 Posting in Blogger

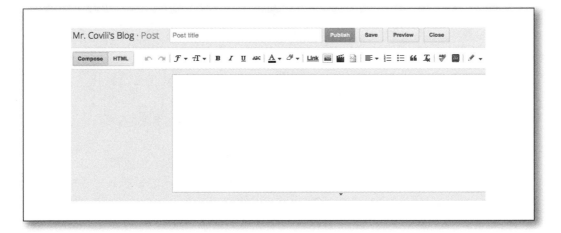

4. Type the body of your post in the provided text editor. The editor should look familiar to you, as it shares several of the same features as Microsoft Word or Open Office.

5. You can changes the **style, size,** and **color** of the fonts.

6. Formatting includes options like **bold, italics,** and **underline.**

7. Once you've typed your post, click the **Publish Post** button to make your comments live.

Adding Multimedia to a Post

The ability to add multimedia to your posts is one of the big differences between blogging and traditional journaling. Creating links, adding pictures, or using video gives the blog a modern twist and engages students so much more than written journals. You can insert different multimedia content into your post using the provided controls. Let's see how it's done.

- Inserting a link in your post (see Figure 5.4:
  1. Highlight the word or phrase you wish to turn into a hyperlink.
  2. To create the link, click on the **Link** option.
  3. A window will open to create the link. Type in the **Text** to display. If you previously highlighted an existing word or phrase in your post, it will appear in the Text field.
  4. Next, provide the URL or web address of the link. You can test the link to ensure you entered the correct information.
  5. Click **OK** when done.

Figure 5.4   Inserting a Link in a Post

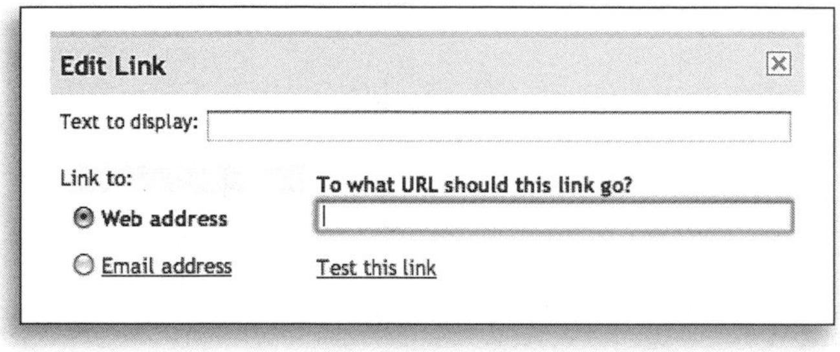

Edit Link   ⊠

Text to display: [   ]

Link to: To what URL should this link go?
◉ Web address   [   ]
○ Email address   Test this link

- Inserting an image in your post:
  1. Select the **Add Image** icon from the toolbar.
  2. A window will open with your choices for adding an image. You can add the image by **Uploading** it to your blog; using an existing image from a previous blog post, including a photo from your Picasa Web Album; or copying the URL of a photo already on the Internet. Photos you use on your blog should either be original, or you should have permission to share the images online.
  3. Once you choose your desired image, click the **Add Selected** button to make the image display in your blog post.
  4. To change the properties of an image once it's in a post, click on the image (see Figure 5.5). You'll be able to change the display size, the alignment, add a caption, or complete a bit of basic editing on the link or image.

Figure 5.5   Setting the Image's Properties

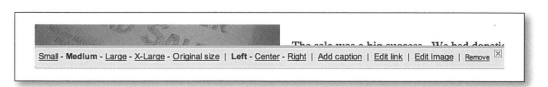

- Inserting a video in your post (see Figure 5.6):
  1. Select the **Add Video** icon in the toolbar.
  2. A window will open with three choices for adding video to your blog. First, you can upload your own video to a post. Or, you can add a

video from YouTube by copying the video's URL. You can also add any of your own videos from YouTube.

Figure 5.6 Uploading or Inserting Video

Videos and images uploaded to your blog are stored by Google in the Picasa Web Album as private content, meaning they are not searchable in the Google database. They do count toward your storage limit in the Picasa Web Album—remember that you get 1 GB of free storage.

Editing a Post and Saving a Draft

Once you've written a post, there may be many occasions when you'll need to reopen the entry to make some revisions (see Figure 5.7). There will be other times when you aren't quite ready to publish a post, so you'll want to save the entry as a draft.

1. On the Dashboard, click the **Posts** button.

2. A list of all your previous posts will appear.

3. Select the desired post and click **Edit.**

This will put you back in the **Post Editor** where you can make the necessary adjustments and republish the post. If your post isn't ready to publish, you'll find a **Save Draft** option next to the Publish button. Even if you don't use the **Save** button, Blogger has an automatic backup on your posts. You should find the system backing up your changes within a few seconds of your typing.

Figure 5.7 Editing a Post

> ☐ **Field Trip on Friday**
> Edit | Delete

Creating Pages for Your Blog

In the past few years, Blogger has added the ability to create stand-alone pages for your blog. It's a great way to have all the features we love about blogging, but also some of the functionality we like about a traditional website. By

Figure 5.8 Creating New Pages in Blogger

Figure 5.9 Arranging Your Pages

creating pages, you can have some information accessible all the time, rather than moving down the blog page as new posts are written on the blog. Here's how to make additional pages on your blog and then build the navigation to them (see Figure 5.8):

1. Click on the **Blogger Options** menu.

2. Select **Pages.**

3. Choose the **New Page** button.

4. The editor will appear very much like the Posting editor. You can use all of the same formatting and content options as you use in your post.

5. Add your content and **Publish** the page to your blog.

6. To choose the layout for the links to your new page, click on the **Show Pages** drop-down menu. You can select to add the links to your new pages along the side of your blog or across the top of your blog (see Figure 5.9).

7. Click on the **Save Arrangement** button at the top right corner of the screen.

■ ADDITIONAL SETUP FOR YOUR CLASSROOM BLOG

Using the Dashboard

When you first log in to Blogger, you'll find yourself on a page called the Dashboard (see Figure 5.10). Think of this page as the hub of your blogging world. From the Dashboard, you can create new blogs, edit existing ones, manage your profile, and learn about updates on the service.

Figure 5.10 The Dashboard in Blogger

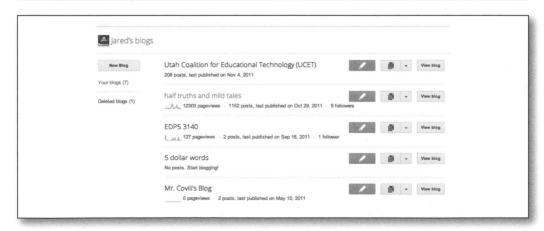

The Dashboard helps you manage all the blogs you have rights to. It's a convenient way to add a new post, change permissions, update the design of your blog, or keep track of your blog's stats.

Some of the quick access links for each blog on your Dashboard include New Post, Blogger Options, and View Blog. You'll find these links are an easy way to jump into your blog and work on the content or customize the functionality.

Blogger Options in the Dashboard

Most of the editing controls are available from the Dashboard. The trick is that they are available from a drop-down menu. When you click on the **Blogger Options** button in the Dashboard, you'll find a host of controls for your blog (see Figure 5.11).

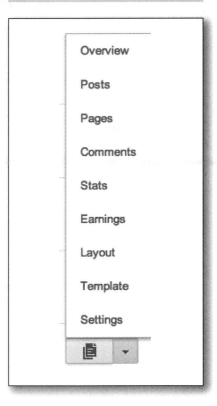

Figure 5.11 Blogger Options Menu

- **Overview:** A quick look at blog features. Learn the latest news from Blogger Buzz. Access tips and tricks as well.
- **Posts:** Create a new post, or edit posts from your archive.
- **Pages:** Allows you to create new pages with static content on your blog.
- **Comments:** Find out what viewers are saying about your posts. You can quickly view readers' comments about your blog.
- **Stats:** Provides users with stats for the blog. See how many visitors have viewed your blog, and find out which posts are most popular.
- **Earnings:** Provides you with reports of earnings if you've chosen to include ads on your blog. This is not something to be concerned about for your classroom blog.
- **Layout:** Customize your blog by adding *Gadgets,* or applications from third party providers, adjusting the column placement on your blog, and more.
- **Template:** Change the look and feel of your blog. Change colors, backgrounds, fonts, and so on.
- **Settings:** You can control all the other elements of your blog here. Change the name or address of your blog, choose permission settings, add more authors, etc.

Using the Template Tab

The Template tab allows you to easily change the look and feel of your blog (see Figure 5.12). People love to give their blog a "one of a kind" look. Changing the look of your blog used to require understanding a bit of HTML or downloading a template from a third-party website. With Blogger in Draft, you have tons of fun options for updating the appearance of your blog.

Changing the Background

1. Click on the **Template** link from the **Blogger Options** button.

2. Choose a new template option.

3. When the Template Designer opens, you'll have a wide variety of choices to **customize** your blog. Pick a different template, change the background image, or pick a new layout. It's up to you. Blogger even gives you a preview window right in the editor, so you can see your changes before applying them to your blog.

4. Click on the **Apply to Blog** button when you're finished.

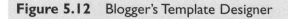

Figure 5.12 Blogger's Template Designer

Adding a Gadget

Gadgets provide you with the ability to customize your blog in many different ways. One of the best things about blogs is how personal they are for their owners. By using gadgets, you can share important information with your users, but you can also give parents and students a little look into some of the fun sides of your classroom and your own personality (see Figure 5.13).

1. Go to your Dashboard and click on **Layout** from the **Blogger Options** button.

2. The **Page Elements** page will load. Here you'll see your current configuration of elements.

3. Click on the **Add a Gadget** link.

4. A window will open with a list of available gadgets for your blog. There are various categories to look at including **basics, featured,** and **most popular.**

Figure 5.13 Add a Gadget from the Menu

5. There are dozens of gadgets to pick from, but the most popular include

   a. Link List—Lets you share links to resources and other popular sites.

   b. Blog roll—For sharing links to your network of colleagues and fellow bloggers.

   c. Pages—For creating static pages for your blog.

   d. Polls—Where you can have students share their opinions. This is a great way to get a quick assessment for your class's views.

   e. Picture or Text—For sharing a favorite image or inspirational quote.

6. In the **Link** window, you need to enter the name of the link and the URL or address for the website.

7. Once you've added the gadget, click the **Save** button in the top right corner of the Page Elements page.

Using the Settings Tab

There are several elements and options available to you in the Setting tab. You can control features related to publishing, e-mailing, commenting, formatting, and more. Rather than explore each of these options, let's focus on the elements that are most important for educators (see Figure 5.14).

Under the **Basic** settings for the blog, you have several different choices to consider, perhaps the most basic of which is deleting the blog. In addition, you

Figure 5.14   Basic Setting Tab

have the option to rename your blog, or change the search settings. If privacy is a concern, then you may want to change your search settings so that your blog is not available for public search. For more on privacy issues, see below.

Permissions for a Blog

As I've taught educators about blogging, one of their biggest concerns is about privacy. They worry about who can post to a blog, who can comment on a blog, and who can view a blog. Teachers should know that Blogger gives you control over all three of these issues and makes changing permissions a snap. Here's how to set limits on posting and reading (see Figure 5.15):

1. Go to your Dashboard and click on the **Blogger Options** button.

2. Choose **Settings** from the menu.

3. In Settings, click on **Basic**.

4. Look for the **Permissions** options.

5. To set limits on reading a blog, under the heading **Blog Readers,** you can select from three options: **Anybody, Only these readers,** or **Only blog authors.**

Figure 5.15   You Choose Who Reads and Edits Your Blog

6. The **Only these readers** option offers the greatest security since you can determine who looks at your blog, though an e-mail invitation. For your class, you can determine the level of security for the blog.

Remember, if you select the "Only these readers" option, no one will be able to read the blog unless you have previously entered his or her e-mail address on an "approved" list.

7. To allow multiple students to collaborate on a single blog, use the **Add Authors** button in the Blog Authors section. You'll be prompted to add an author by providing their e-mail address as verification.

Using these privacy settings is a useful way to have students work with one another, but maintain a level of personal privacy that's important to their parents and to the school.

Comments and Your Blog

Comments are one of the key elements that transform a basic website into a collaborative blog. For your classroom blog, you will want to allow students to make comments on your posts. This will enable a discussion about information and ideas, versus an announcement from the teacher. However, while we want to encourage comments, we still need to have some control over who can make comments and how we can monitor the discussion. To manage these settings for your blog, do the following:

1. Go to **Settings.**

2. Click on **Posts and Comments.**

3. You need to decide **Who Can Comment** on your blog. There are four choices:

   a. Anyone—This is the least secure option, as anonymous readers can leave comments on your blog.

   b. Registered Users—This allows anyone with a Google account or an Open ID account to comment.

   c. Users with Google accounts—This allows just those with a Google account to comment.

   d. Only Members of this Blog—Only those who've been invited using their e-mail address are allowed to comment. This is the most secure and a favorite option of many schools.

4. Next, be sure to decide on **Comment Moderation.** There are different choices for this setting, but choosing to moderate comments means that the thoughts can only appear on the blog if you approve them.

Figure 5.16 Comment Moderation Helps You Control the Content

Comment moderation
- ○ Always
- ○ Only on posts older than [14] days
- ● Never

The advantage of comment moderation is that you control what is posted to the blog (see Figure 5.16). You can ensure that nothing inappropriate is said and that all the comments relate to the topic. The downside is that you lose the spontaneity and immediacy that students love about blogs. It's very engaging for students to hit "post" and then immediately see their comments as part of the blog.

5. There is one last option to enable on your blog—**Word Verification.** I know many of you don't like it when you have to type those crazy letters that appear in a box when you go to make comments on a blog or site, but it prevents blog comments from being hit by spammers. By enabling Word Verification, you ensure that computers cannot auto-post inappropriate content to your classroom blog.

6. Once you've finished setting the comment options on your blog, select **Save Settings,** and you're done.

MORE IDEAS FOR GOING GOOGLE

Classroom Ideas for Blogging

- Student writing journals—Have your students create a daily writing journal as a way to work on their writing skills and share their thoughts. The blogs can be private, so they are only available to the student and the teacher. This provides the students with a modern twist on the notebook journal they may already be using.
- Student portfolios—We mentioned this project as part of the Google Sites section of this book, but you can also use Blogger for creating a student portfolio. It's a great way to focus on reflection for the different learning goals in the portfolio, but it is a bit more difficult to include artifacts.

TIPS FOR THE GOOGLE CLASSROOM

- Google has made several changes to Blogger over the past several months. If your version of Blogger looks different from the one depicted here, click on the **Use the New Version** option on the Dashboard.
- Think about maintaining a blog in which you discuss educational issues. With all the demands that are placed upon teachers, I know this can sound like "one more thing," but sharing your thoughts on education can be a great release for a lot of the stress of teaching. It also provides a way to join in the conversation and share your insights. Start slowly, and don't feel obligated to blog on a daily basis. Share at your own pace.
- I mentioned that blogs are part of many educators' PLN (personal learning network). Some great blogs to consider reading if you're interested in educational issues include the following:

  o Two Cents Worth (http://davidwarlick.com/2cents/)
  o Weblogg-ed (http://weblogg-ed.com/)
  o Cool Cat Teacher (http://coolcatteacher.blogspot.com/)
  o Drape's Takes (http://drapestakes.blogspot.com/)
  o dy/dan (http://blog.mrmeyer.com/)

- Public versus private blogging—I know this is the big debate in blogging circles, but I would argue on the side of public blogging. Part of the magic of blogging is that the conversation is available as part of an open blog. In the classroom, you'll need to establish clear guidelines for student posting, and you'll need to follow your district's legal guidelines for web content, but sharing comments publicly is one of the best things about blogging.

6

Google Groups

FIVE THINGS TO KNOW ABOUT GOOGLE GROUPS

1. You can create your own group or join an existing group.
2. Messages can come to your e-mail.
3. Teachers can create student-led groups.
4. Projects can include creating a class discussion board or having international pen pals.
5. Google Groups can translate other languages into English.

Google Groups is an easy and effective way to communicate with parents and students. You can create groups for the parents to talk with one another about events in the classroom, a student study group can improve achievement, or you can even develop a support group for you and your colleagues.

Google Groups is a free online site that helps groups of people easily share information and communicate with each other. Groups can be public or private places where members share files, post ideas, and conduct discussions either on the web or via e-mail.

> **NETS-S Standard 3 Objective c**
>
> Teachers communicate relevant information and ideas effectively to students, parents, and peers using a variety of digital-age media and formats. (ISTE, 2007)

Think of Google Groups as the information center of your classroom. Unlike a traditional website; however, the communication can take place between and among all the different groups within your classroom—parents, students, and from you to each of these groups.

CREATING A GROUP ■

There are several different ways in which you can use your Google Group. As we've already seen, a Google Group is a great way to have a dialogue with students, parents, or colleagues. Let's set up a group together and see what it requires (see Figure 6.1).

Create a group...

1. Go to groups.google.com.

2. Select the **Create a group** button.

3. A form will appear, providing you with the necessary information for creating your group. You'll need to

   a. Name your group

   b. Create an e-mail address for your group. This will be used to facilitate the discussion aspects of Google Groups.

   c. Provide a brief description of your group. This will help parents, students, and colleagues know they have found the correct group to join.

   d. Choose the level of access. There are three different options:

      i. **Public**—Anyone can join the group and read the archives.

      ii. **Announcement only**—The archives of your discussion board are public, but only those with permission can post messages.

      iii. **Restricted**—Only those invited may participate in groups. This is the most popular setting for schools, and it provides the greatest level of privacy.

4. Select the **Create my group** button.

5. Next, let's add members to our new group.

Figure 6.1 Setting Up Your Google Group

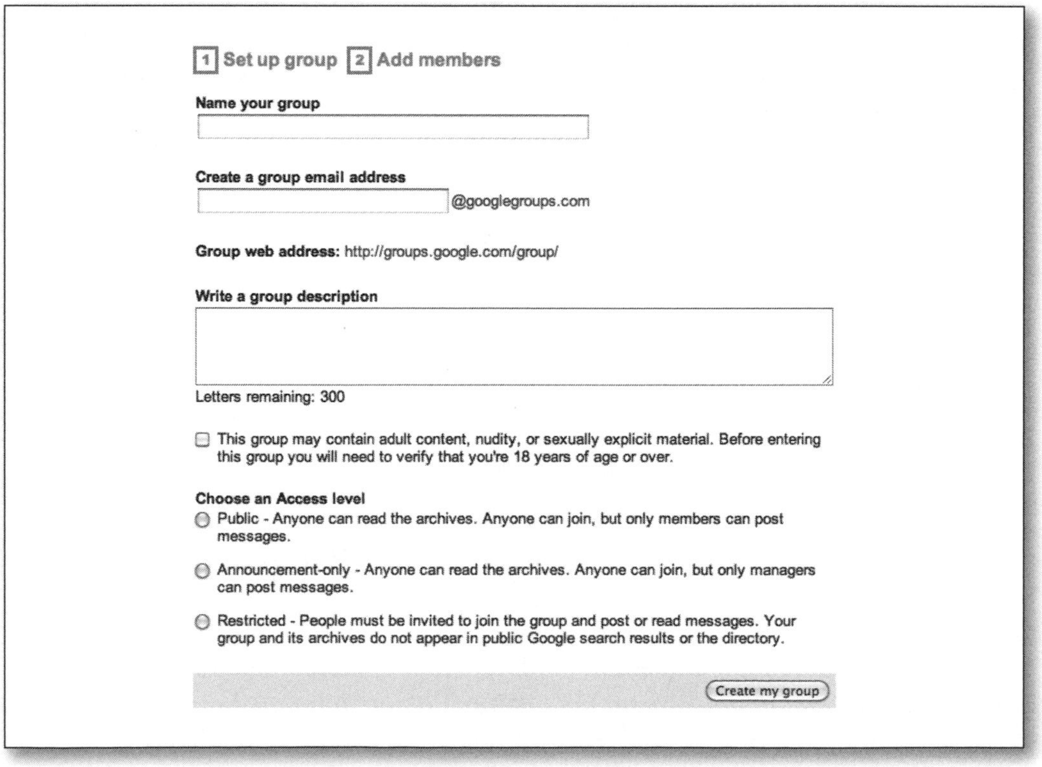

1 Set up group 2 Add members

Name your group

Create a group email address
@googlegroups.com

Group web address: http://groups.google.com/group/

Write a group description

Letters remaining: 300

☐ This group may contain adult content, nudity, or sexually explicit material. Before entering this group you will need to verify that you're 18 years of age or over.

Choose an Access level

○ Public - Anyone can read the archives. Anyone can join, but only members can post messages.

○ Announcement-only - Anyone can read the archives. Anyone can join, but only managers can post messages.

○ Restricted - People must be invited to join the group and post or read messages. Your group and its archives do not appear in public Google search results or the directory.

Create my group

6. You have two choices for adding new members—invite them to join the group by e-mail, or add them directly.

   a. By inviting others to join your group, they will receive an e-mail that details the group's basic information. Your recipient will have the choice to join the group or not. He or she can also choose what level of participation to have in the group.

   b. Add people to your group directly. By entering in an e-mail address directly, you automatically enroll someone in your group. This is a great option for a teacher with his or her students, but you wouldn't want to enroll parents automatically for a group without checking with them first.

STARTING A NEW DISCUSSION ■

Creating a new discussion in Google Groups is as simple as clicking the **New Topic** button (see Figure 6.2). The post editor window will open, and you can create your post using a standard word processing editor. This should look familiar, as it is the same format as in Blogger and Google Sites.

Figure 6.2 Creating a Topic in Google Groups

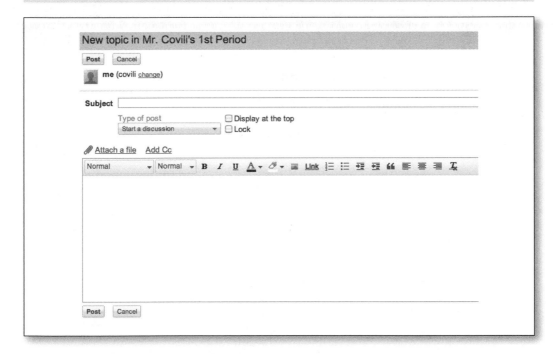

Be sure to type a **Subject** that provides insight as to the topic of your post, and when you're finished, click on the **Post** button.

It's time to let the discussion begin, as all group members will receive your message as part of the group. After your comments have been shared, you'll find that replies to your post will be threaded as part of the discussion board.

Changing Your Groups' Settings

You can customize the settings for your group: Indicate who will have permission to create topics or post messages, set the online appearance of your group, or establish a default signature for all messages from your group.

Figure 6.3 Finding the Settings Link

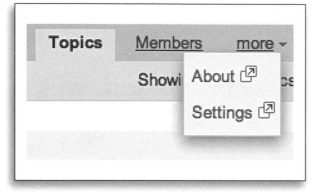

1. Go into the **Settings** link found under the **More** heading in the top right corner of your Groups screen.

2. Under the **General** link, you'll find the ability to adjust the basic options for your group.

3. In **Access,** you can determine the level of permissions for the group.

4. To delete a group, click on the **Advanced** link.

5. Click on the **Appearance** link. You can change the color, the layout, even the icon for your group. Use the default icons or upload one of your own.

Project Idea: Create a Discussion Board for Parents

NETS-S Standard 3 Objective c

Teachers communicate relevant information and ideas effectively to students, parents, and peers using a variety of digital-age media and formats. (ISTE, 2007)

Create a discussion board of topics to be shared with the parents of your students. This is a great way for you to communicate with all the parents directly, but it also allows the parents to communicate with one another as well.

One of best parts of using Google Groups is that messages can be received in each individual's e-mail box. Think about it: Parents don't even have to leave their computer to be part of the group! The topics will show up as a threaded discussion, so you'll quickly see the entire dialogue in a convenient location (see Figure 6.4).

Another benefit of using Google Groups for this discussion board is that parents can choose how often they want to receive messages (see Figure 6.5). They can choose from the following options:

- **No Email**—They can only access the group on the Internet.
- **Abridged Email**—They will receive one summarized e-mail per day.
- **Digest Email**—They will see a compilation of new messages each day.
- **Email**—They can read each new message in their e-mail.

Parents can choose how involved they want to be with the discussion board. The key is that they have options for their involvement.

Figure 6.4 Threaded Messages in a Group

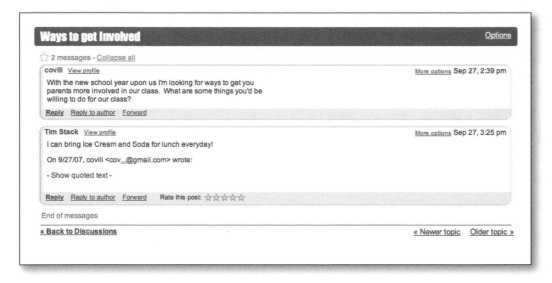

Figure 6.5 Options for Receiving Messages in a Group

Project Idea: Student Group With International Students

One of the newest features in Google Groups is a language translation tool. This means you can have members of your group from different countries and cultures, but all the responses can be read in your students' native tongues.

When a message is posted in Google Group in a language other than English, Google will offer to **Translate message to English** (see Figure 6.6).

Once you've had Google Groups translate the message, you'll find both the original message and the translation available to you. Groups will also ask if you want all future messages in that language to be translated as well (see Figure 6.7).

NETS-S Standard 2 Objective c

Students use digital media and environments to communicate and work collaboratively, including at a distance, to support individual learning and contribute to the learning of others. Students develop cultural understanding and global awareness by engaging with learners of other cultures. (ISTE, 2007)

Google Groups can help you find possible classrooms from different countries that might want to join your group.

1. From the Google Groups homepage, click on the **Browse all Groups** button.
2. Several categories of groups will appear. Select the **Schools and Universities** category.
3. Next, you can choose which grade levels you're looking for. You can choose from **University, Primary schools,** and **Secondary schools.**
4. You'll be prompted to choose from different regions of the world. Click on the region you're interested in.
5. A list of existing groups will appear. You can contact the administrator of the group and set up a possible **Pen Pal** group between your classes.

Figure 6.6 Translate Messages Into English

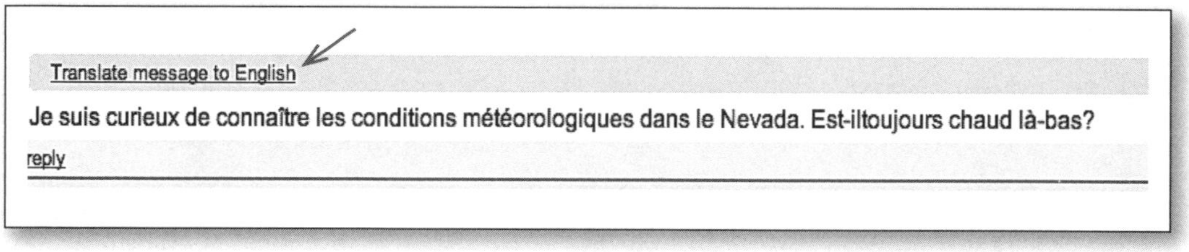

Translate message to English
Je suis curieux de connaître les conditions météorologiques dans le Nevada. Est-iltoujours chaud là-bas?
reply

Figure 6.7 You Can Translate All Future Messages in a Thread

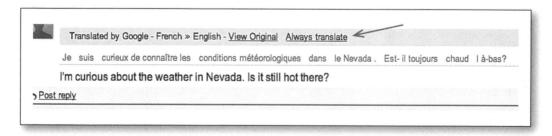

Translated by Google - French » English - View Original Always translate
Je suis curieux de connaître les conditions météorologiques dans le Nevada . Est- il toujours chaud l à-bas?
I'm curious about the weather in Nevada. Is it still hot there?
Post reply

Participating in an international group is a great way to have your students learn from others around the world. It's a modern example of the pen pals many of us had when we were in school.

MORE IDEAS FOR GOING GOOGLE

Additional Ideas for Google Groups

- Have students create their own study group—They can use the group for class projects, homework assignments, or just to talk about what's going on in class. The group provides a structured way for students to work with one another.
- Take your classroom discussions online—Groups can be an effective way to introduce an online component to your classes. By having some of your discussion online, you'll give yourself a bit of extra classroom time for activities, and you'll provide your students with an online experience.
- Create a private group for school clubs or sports teams to share the latest news, announcements, and pictures—This is a good tool for building community and keeping parents/students up-to-date on what's going on with your club or team.

TIPS FOR THE GOOGLE CLASSROOM

- Remember, Google Groups doesn't work alone. Include the link to your group on your Google Site, and provide the students with plenty of opportunities to contribute to the discussion.
- You and your students can be part of multiple groups. Have the kids make their own group for any projects they may work on with partners or small teams.
- Think about expanding your personal learning network by joining different public Google Groups. There are several groups dealing with educational issues. There's a group for teachers who use Google tools in their classrooms—it's a great resource for finding lesson plan ideas.

7

Google+

❧❧

FIVE THINGS TO KNOW ABOUT GOOGLE+

1. Contacts are organized into "circles."
2. You can send information to all your circles or choose specific circles.
3. Creating a "hangout" provides you with access to video chat with members.
4. You can quickly share content with circles using Google+ buttons for your browser.
5. Google+ is open to everyone—no need to be invited.

❧❧

The latest Google tool is Google+, a social media tool that can be used for communicating and collaborating with students, parents, and colleagues. It follows the Facebook model, which allows individuals to add friends, thus granting them access to shared content. Google+ can certainly help you as you look to expand your social circles, but it has some intriguing possibilities for schools. Let's take a closer look.

WHY USE GOOGLE+? ■

Student Collaboration

"Circles" will allow students to create groups for collaborative projects. With "hangouts," the students will then be able to meet virtually to work on their project, share information, and provide feedback to each other (these terms are discussed further below). You can use Google+ as a way to facilitate anything from writing groups to study partners.

Online and Blended Classrooms

Google + provides teachers with additional options beyond the traditional brick and mortar of the classroom. With Google+, teachers can have their students work in online or blended environments by creating *hangouts*—private video chat rooms. Up to 10 students can collaborate at once using Google+ to facilitate the meeting.

Staff Professional Development

Professional development could also be done through hangouts. Principals could have various professional learning circles within the building, and hangouts can provide the online space to share lots of different content with one another. It's a great way to get teachers together, without having to schedule the library (Curtis, 2011)!

■ GETTING STARTED IN GOOGLE+

To begin using Google+, do the following:

1. Go to plus.google.com, or click on the **+You** icon in the top left corner of the Google homepage.

2. Sign in with your Google account.

Features in Google+

Google+ includes the following features (see Figure 7.1):

Figure 7.1   Features in Google+

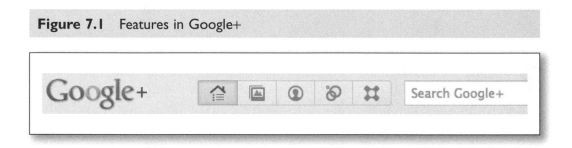

Stream

This is the homepage for Google+. On the Stream page, you'll find updates from all of your contacts. The stream is organized chronologically, so newer content will add to the top of the page as older content moves toward the bottom.

Photos

You have the ability to upload your photos and share them with contacts in Google+. Google provides you with 2 GB of storage for your images. If you're already using Picasa Web Album, you'll find those photos are already available in Google+.

Circles

Circles allow you to group your contact together based upon your relationship with them (see Figure 7.2). For example, you can create a circle for all the parents of your third-grade class. When you post something to Google+, you can filter the recipient list, which means your Parents group won't read posts intended for your friends. This is a great way to keep personal information personal.

You can also share contacts between circles, which provides you with a great deal of flexibility in contacting just the right group of individuals.

Circles are one of the biggest changes from other social network sites, and this is one of the features that makes Google+ appealing to schools. Circles will allow what educational consultant Tom Barnett (2011) calls "targeted sharing," something that will be very useful for specific classes and topics.

Hangouts

Hangouts allow multiple contacts to enter into a live video chat room. Where programs like Skype allows for one-to-one video chats for free, Google+ will let you talk with up to 10 of your contacts at once.

Messenger

This feature allows you and your students a quick way to message several people. Rather than sending a message multiple times, simply send an entire group one message at one time.

Quick Sharing With Google+

Google + provides you with a toolbar for the browser that allows for quick sharing with different circles (see Figure 7.3). Click on the **Share** button from Google.com, and you can add comments, photos, links, videos, or locations.

Figure 7.2   Organize Contacts Into Circles

Figure 7.3   Quick Share Your Content on Google+

Project Idea: Creating a Hangout for a Student Study Group

A hangout can be a fun way to get your students collaborating in small groups. Hangouts have plenty of options including IM (instant messaging) or video chat, live video streaming from YouTube, and more.

To Create a Hangout

To create a hangout, take the following steps (see Figure 7.4):

Figure 7.4 Start a Hangout

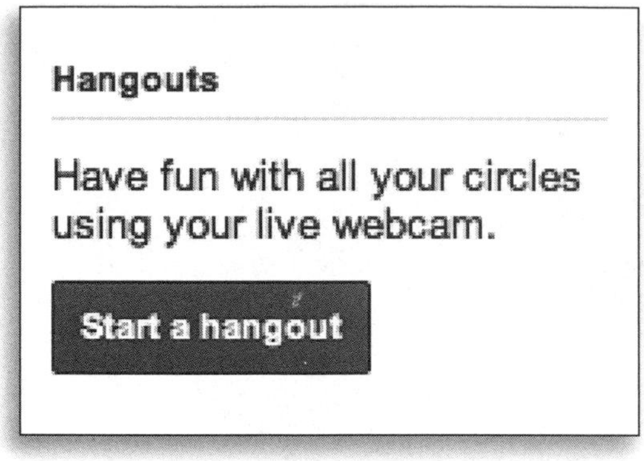

Hangouts

Have fun with all your circles using your live webcam.

Start a hangout

1. Click on the **Start a Hangout** button. It's found on the lower right of the Stream screen.

2. You'll be prompted to add members of a particular circle of your contacts to the hangout, or you can enter in specific e-mail addresses.

3. Once you invite others to join the hangout, you'll have to wait for them to accept your invitation.

4. After they join the hangout, you're all set. You should see a split screen of all participants along the bottom of the room and a larger shared canvas for video chatting with one another.

5. You can adjust the settings to display your video or improve your audio. Those buttons are found along the lower right side of the hangout room.

Enabling Chat or YouTube Video Playback

- To add a live chat to your hangout, click on the **Chat** button, found in the lower left corner of your hangout room.
- You can start instant messaging the group.
- For video, click on the **YouTube** button, also located along the lower left side of the hangout room.
- You can perform a YouTube search to find the right clip.
- While the video is playing, your group can still discuss the content through your microphones or by using the IM chat (see Figure 7.5).

Figure 7.5 Share YouTube Videos in Hangout

MORE IDEAS FOR GOING GOOGLE

- Bring in a guest presenter—Google Hangouts provide you with the opportunity to bring in guest presenters to your classroom. With the ability to have multiple people in a hangout, you can bring in presenters from around the world to share with your students.
- Try a classroom film festival—While in Hangouts, students can watch YouTube videos and chat about them. Have your students create movies they can share through YouTube and start your own film festival in Google+.

TIPS FOR THE GOOGLE CLASSROOM

- Google + is designed to create many different circles within your contact list. Be sure to take advantage of this feature by adding circles of students, parents, and colleagues.
- Privacy is always a big concern with students. Google + allows students the option to add adults to their circles without having to become a contact in the adults' Google+ account.

Part II

Creativity and Innovation

Today's students are speaking out to their teachers loudly and clearly: They want activities and assignments in school that allow them to create content and share it with others. Unfortunately, kids still find that much of school involves passive learning. It is time spent listening to teachers lecture from the front of the classroom.

> So much of school is still talking to kids. Presenting, telling, explaining to the whole class and when kids hear that they just fall asleep. They tune out. Smart kids, they say after five minutes I go to sleep. What the kids want to do is the group work, it's the project work, and it's the casework. They want to share things. They know they are world citizens. They want to affect the world. (Prensky, 2010, n.p.)

As we move into 21st century classrooms, our curriculum must reflect the changes technology affords us. Worksheets and reports still have a place in today's classrooms, but they need to be supplemented with multimedia projects. Activities involving digital images with Picasa, video creation and distribution with YouTube, and innovative multimedia tools like Google Earth move students along the levels of Bloom's Taxonomy and encourage high levels of creativity and critical thinking. Projects provide students with the opportunity to "show what they know."

> Media is the language of kids. Students who may not take to learning by reading a textbook or listening to a lecture often jump at the chance to understand complex concepts by presenting finished products in the form of a film or a Web documentary or a Microsoft PowerPoint presentation. (Edutopia, n.d., n.p.)

In looking at 21st century learning skills, student projects that involve multimedia encourage students to think creatively, utilizing a wide array of tools to create and innovate. Students may not always readily admit it, but they want to be challenged. When kids are given opportunities to grow and develop their ideas, they want to

- Create new and worthwhile ideas (both incremental and radical concepts).
- Elaborate, refine, analyze and evaluate their own ideas in order to improve and maximize creative efforts.
- Develop, implement and communicate new ideas to others effectively.
- Demonstrate originality and inventiveness in work and understand the real world limits to adopting new ideas. (Partnership for 21st Century Skills, 2004, n.p.)

■ GOOGLE'S IMPACT ON CREATIVITY AND INNOVATION

Authentic assessment requires global distribution.

—Tyson, 2009

I heard this statement from Dr. Tim Tyson, and it stopped me in my tracks. Why global distribution? American schools don't really have a global perspective, so his comment challenged my way of thinking. As I pondered on his intent, it really hit home with me.

Kids want to create projects and share them with an audience. In schools, it is usually an audience of one—the teacher. This really doesn't provide much motivation. Think about it: You put tons of time into an assignment, and the only person who sees it isn't one of your peers; it's an adult. The only type of validation you get from the hours of work is a grade? An "A" doesn't really mean anything to some kids.

Now, let's look at what the kids are doing when they aren't in school. Many spend countless days and nights working on a video, a song, a dance, and the minute they think they have it perfected, where does it end up? YouTube. Why? So everyone they know can see it. Even perfect strangers can view the video and make comments about it. Kids feel important, and they know they are making a contribution that's valued. Remember, authentic assessment requires global distribution, and Google tools provide just that platform for kids.

■ DOES SCHOOL REFLECT THE "REAL WORLD"?

So much of students' experience outside of school differs from what life is like in the classroom. While technology dominates much of our kids' attention at home, school seems to be a vacuum—a place where students' experience and know-how seem to be devalued. This fact isn't lost on our leaders. In the National Education Technology Plan (NETP) 2010, the problem is addressed as follows:

Many students' lives today are filled with technology that gives them mobile access to information and resources 24/7, enables them to create multimedia content and share it with the world, and allows them to participate in online social networks where people from all over the world share ideas, collaborate, and learn new things. Outside school, students are free to pursue their passions in their own way and at their own pace. The opportunities are limitless, borderless, and instantaneous.

The challenge for our education system is to leverage the learning sciences and modern technology to create engaging, relevant, and personalized learning experiences for all learners that mirror students' daily lives and the reality of their futures. In contrast to traditional classroom instruction, this requires that we put students at the center and empower them to take control of their own learning by providing flexibility on several dimensions. (U.S. Department of Education, 2010, n.p.)

Students need to be able to share their multimedia projects with others. It doesn't always have to be on YouTube or Facebook, but there needs to be a forum where students feel their work matters. Technology is a great facilitator of sharing content, and Google tools make creating and sharing projects easier than ever.

In this section, we'll focus on three tools that promote creativity and innovation: Google Earth, Picasa/Picasa Web Album, and YouTube. Each of these programs provides opportunities for project-based learning and encourages students to creatively develop innovative assignments.

8

Google Earth

FIVE THINGS TO KNOW ABOUT GOOGLE EARTH

1. Google Earth uses aerial maps to create a free interactive map of the world.
2. The Layers panel provides access to multimedia content from around the web.
3. Google Earth provides real-time data from places around the world.
4. Students can create multimedia virtual tours of locations all over the globe.
5. Google Earth files are known as KML or KMZ, and they can be found using a Google Advanced Search.

The program Google Earth dramatically transformed the way in which we see the world. It brought maps into the foreground on our computers and made cartography seem somewhat cool. You didn't need to know the names of tiny countries to be able to find them in Google Earth. You could simply search for a region and fly in to all the amazing sites from around the globe. Instantly, kids were playing with maps—can you believe it?

Google Earth utilizes aerial photos of the entire world to create a new kind of map, a digital map—a map that allows you to zoom in to almost any location on Earth and virtually experience the world from a first-person point of view. But Google Earth is more than just a basic map; it provides the user with a realistic look at places from the ground as well as the air. Google Earth gives such an incredibly detailed view of the world, you may never need a passport again!

For teachers, Google Earth has been a revelation: a free tool that provides content and images of countries around the globe. Since it is such a visual program, it can be used by students of all ages. Before Google Earth, maps were seen by kids as old and boring—typically, something controlled by the teacher at the front of the room. Once Google Earth was developed,

> **NETS-S Standard 1 Objective c**
>
> Students demonstrate creative thinking, construct knowledge, and develop innovative products and processes using technology. Students use models and simulations to explore complex systems and issues. (ISTE, 2007)

an innovative pedagogical shift occurred. Now it was the *students* in control of what they looked at on the map. They literally could see the world, and they loved it.

One of the biggest misconceptions about Google Earth is that the tool is really only valuable for geography and social studies teachers. This couldn't be more false. Teachers from almost any discipline can use Google Earth as a way to open the real world to their students. Anne Brusca, a Library Media Specialist from Center Street Elementary in New York, noticed how engaged all her fifth-grade students were when they used Google Earth to take a virtual tour of locations from the book *Orphan Train.* "I've never seen them so intent," she says. "This got them to deeper learning" (quoted in Boss, n.d.-b, n.p.).

■ GETTING STARTED WITH GOOGLE EARTH

Unlike many of the tools we've examined thus far, Google Earth has both an online and a download version. The online version of Google Earth is fairly new. It utilizes the same search feature as the download version, but most classrooms focus on using the original download version of the program because there's so much more information available. For the purposes of our discussion, we're going to focus on the download version of Google Earth, but feel free to check out the online version at http://maps.google.com—click on the link for **Earth** in the upper right corner of the screen.

To download Google Earth,

1. Go to http://earth.google.com.

2. Click on the big blue **Download** button.

3. Since Google Earth is a program you run and store on your computer, you'll need to be sure your computer meets the system requirements. Basically, you need to be running Windows XP, Vista, or Windows 7 if you're on a PC, and Mac OS 10.5 or later if you're using a Mac. For a complete list of system requirements, check out http://earth.google.com/support/bin/answer.py?hl=en&answer=20701

4. After the download, the installation is no different from any other program. Follow the wizard, and within a few minutes you'll be up and running on Google Earth.

■ GOOGLE EARTH BASICS

Navigation

Google Earth has a set of navigation controls going down the right side of the screen. Now, you may not see these tools all the time. When not in use or in contact with the cursor, the navigation controls actually disappear into the background of the program. How cool is that? To make the navigation reappear, just hover your mouse over the top right corner of the screen. Here are a few basic tools in the navigation controls.

- Look Joystick: This tool allows you to look at a location from different perspectives. You'll notice the control has an eyeball in the center of it, giving you the impression that you should use this tool to look around the screen. By clicking on any of the arrows on the joystick, you'll be able to change your vantage point.
- Move Joystick: Use this when you want to move around the screen. Located below the look joystick, this tool allows you to slide around on the screen. You can use the arrow keys along the outside of the dial, or you can use the arrows keys on the keyboard directly. One other trick is to left click on the screen, and drag your cursor to another location on the map. This will center that location on the map.
- Zoom Slider: This slider allows you to zoom in on a location. You can go from a global perspective looking straight down to looking at an individual house from street level. In addition to using the slider, you can also narrow or broaden your focus by using the scroll wheel in your mouse. Zooming is an effective way for students to narrow their attention and bring different elements into focus.

Figure 8.1 Navigation Controls in Google Earth

Search

Google Earth has three major search tools to help you navigate around the world. Let's take a closer look at how each one works. (See Figure 8.2.)

- Fly To: This is how you and your students will travel to locations around the globe.
  - o Enter in a landmark, an address, a city, country, or even latitude and longitude coordinates if you know them.
  - o The more detail you provide, the better chance you have to reach your destination.
  - o Once you've entered your desired location, click on the magnifying glass, and you should be "flying,"
- Find Businesses: Using this feature, students can locate all the different services available near a desired location. This is great if you're having kids identify local businesses they have access to when studying a location. One local teacher created a great activity where

Figure 8.2 Using Search in Google Earth

▼ Search

| Fly To | Find Businesses | Directions |

Fly to e.g., New York, NY

her kindergarten students found the community services (e.g., police station, fire station, supermarket) they had recently visited as part of their class fieldtrips.

- Directions: Type in two locations, and Google Earth will calculate your trip and travel time. The information is based on "turn-by-turn" driving directions. You may never get lost again! Directions is a fun feature to help students understand distance and location.

An effective activity for younger students is to have them find a safe walking route to school from their homes. The kids can look at the names of the different streets as they virtually travel from their house to the school.

Places

Places is Google Earth's storage bin for saved locations on the map. You can create your own saved locations using the tools in Google Earth, or you can download saved location files from the Internet and add them to your own version of Google Earth. Once a location is either saved in or added to Google Earth, you'll find it in the Places menu. Let's look at taking an interactive field trip in Google Earth using the Places section (see Figure 8.3).

1. Go to the **Places** section of the menu.

2. Click on the drop-down arrow to the right of the Places folder.

3. Here you'll find the **Sightseeing** folder. It contains premade trips to some of the world's most amazing locations. Click on the **Sightseeing** drop-down menu and browse the available choices.

4. Double-click on the name of your desired location, and you'll fly to that destination.

Figure 8.3 Using the Places Section of Google Earth

You'll find everything from the Grand Canyon to Red Square as possible travel destinations. This is an amazing way to view areas up close and personal. Instead of simply looking down on the Grand Canyon, you'll literally be flying in between the rock walls along the Colorado River. It's as close as you'll come to the canyon without going there and hiring a tour guide! Can you imagine guiding your class of second graders through the Grand Canyon while exploring the various types of rock you'll see on your journey? Talk about real-world activities!

"We go to places like Mount St. Helens, so we can see the devastation there," says Diane King, a fifth-grade science teacher at Lakeview Elementary School in St. Cloud, Florida. "We go to the Grand Canyon. We fly over the San Andreas Fault, and you can actually see the fault line. Anything we're learning about, we'll just fly there" (quoted in Standen, n.d., n.p.).

Places is also the primary folder for any locations you choose to save in Google Earth. We'll get more into this in a bit, but Google Earth allows you to mark and save locations around the globe for a customized view of your world. Once a location is saved, you'll find the information in the Places folder.

In addition to saving your own locations in Google Earth, you can download locations others have marked and save them in your Places folder. For teachers, this means you can search for locations dealing with various curriculum topics you teach.

FINDING LOCATION FILES OR ■
VIRTUAL TOURS FOR GOOGLE EARTH

None of us has enough time to find or create all the resources we need in the classroom. This is particularly true when using Google Earth. To make it easier on yourself, rather than creating an interactive tour for each of your lessons, try searching the Google database for Google Earth tours and location markers your teaching colleagues have already created.

When trying to find educational virtual tours for Google Earth, there are three primary methods: Advanced Google Search, the Google Earth Community, and the Google Earth Gallery. Let's look at each of these tools.

Using Google's Advanced Search

1. Go to the Google homepage at www.google.com.

2. Click on the **Advanced Search** link on the lower right side of the Search box.

3. Scroll down the options look for the field titled **File type.** Here you'll find a drop-down menu that provides you with a list of various types of searchable files.

Figure 8.4   Finding KMZ Files Using Advanced Search

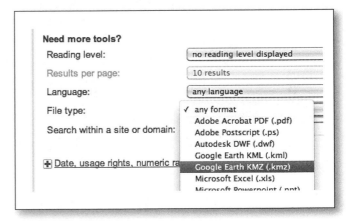

There are two Google Earth file types you can find online, KML and KMZ. Both types of files can contain location, descriptions, and embedded information in online content; the key difference between the file types is that KMZ files are compressed into a zipped format, so there can be more stored information and multiple locations (see Figure 8.4).

Using Google Earth Community

1. In Google Earth, click on the **Help** menu.

2. Select the **Google Earth Community.**

In the Google Earth Community database, you'll find a direct link to the vast amount of information the community provides. A great part of the Google Earth Community for teachers is that there is a dedicated area specifically for education (see Figure 8.5).

Figure 8.5 Google Earth Community for Education

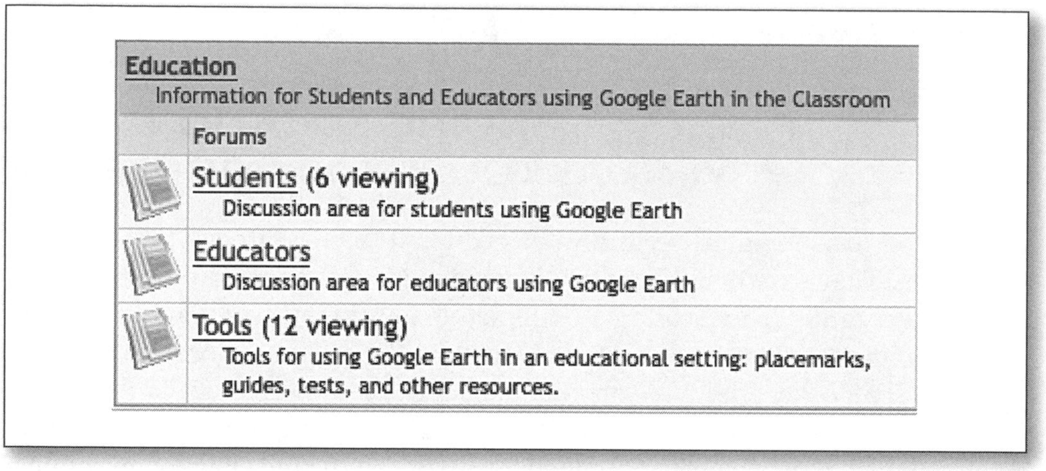

In addition to having numerous educational virtual tours stored in it, the Google Earth Community provides teachers and students with a forum to share ideas for implementing Google Earth in their assignments. There are also many available educational tools in Google Earth found in the Google Earth Community.

Remember, the education world has tons of tools just waiting for you to access. Once you know where to look for them, Google Earth can transform from a basic search tool into a multimedia treasure chest.

Using the Google Earth Gallery

1. In Google Earth, click on the **Layers** panel.

2. Select the **Earth Gallery** link.

Another good place to find Google Earth resources is in Google Earth itself. Located at the top of the Layers panel, the **Earth Gallery** link takes you directly into the public gallery on earth.google.com. There are several different galleries available at this site, but the best one for our purposes is the **Educational gallery.**

In the educational gallery, you'll find KMZ files covering a variety of subjects and curriculum areas, such as the following.

- Science: Find information about topics including real-time earthquakes, global climate change, and oil spills.
- Social Studies: Access information about historical sites, census data from around the world, and political campaign results from recent elections.

- There are also biographical sketches of some famous people, and you can take a peek at the different Major League Baseball stadiums. The gallery is constantly growing, and it's a good starting point for a fun Google Earth research project.

LAYERS ■

The Layers panel is the hidden gem of Google Earth. This is the section that turns Google Earth from a normal 3D map into an interactive information center. As you "turn on" various layers, you have visual access to information from tons of different sources, utilizing multiple areas of the core curriculum (see Figure 8.6).

Each of these layers will display on your Google Earth map, and they provide unique content about sources from around the globe. As a teacher, this provides you with the opportunity to share information, and it allows your students to draw connections to the content they are learning in class.

"It has kids make realizations based on observations they make," says Aidan Chopra, an education program manager at Google, "and that's really the gold standard in education. There are no conclusions in Google Earth; there are trillions of pieces of information out there that students can use to form their own conclusions. A good teacher can then build on those observations and guide them to meet the class's learning objectives" (Standen, n.d., n.p.).

Let's take a closer look at some of the "layers" in Google Earth and explore the various ways in which you can use this information as part of your curriculum. Access the **Layers** panel at the bottom of the menu toolbar along the left side of Google Earth.

Figure 8.6 Using the Layers Panel

Finding Your Way Around

There are a few layers specifically designed to help with identifying places on the map. These include **Borders and Labels, Places,** and **Roads.**

- Borders and Labels: This layer will display geographic boundaries such as state lines and country borders, as well as geographic features like rivers, mountains, lakes, and so on.
- Places: This layer displays city, state, and country names.
- Roads: Turning on this layer helps students find their way around on the local level, by displaying the names of roads on the map.

For a fun look at the White House, be sure and turn on the Roads layer to ensure the address really is 1600 Pennsylvania Ave!

Enabling the Roads layers can also help younger students recognize areas around the school. We mentioned earlier the idea of having students create a walking route from their homes to the school. You can do that far more easily using the Roads layer.

Viewing the World Differently

Google Earth has several layers that can help your students see the world around them using innovative model, photo, and video layers. Let's explore a handful of these visual layers including 3D Buildings, Street View, Photos, Gigapan/GigaPixl, and YouTube. As you turn on these different layers, Google Earth will display a wide array of visual content to help your students view their world differently.

3D Buildings turns Google Earth from an average mapping program into a transformative tool, one that changes the way in which we view our world. Imagine scrolling across the countryside and then encountering the Coliseum rising from the ground in the heart of Rome. Take a trip to New York and have your students view the Statue of Liberty for the first time.

Google Earth has hundreds of three-dimensional models you can access by using the Layers panel. In the 3D Buildings layer, your students can access models of local buildings, including government and civic centers, but also famous landmarks and cultural icons. Now, much of this content is user created, so you won't find a 3D model of everything you'll see in reality. Still, your students can get up close to such landmarks as the Golden Gate Bridge, the Great Wall of China, the Eiffel Tower, and many others.

Figure 8.7   Viewing Buildings Using the 3D Buildings Layer

I'm always amazed when using Google Earth to take students to Washington, D.C., to look at the White House for the first time (see Figure 8.7). The aerial photos are impressive at first glance, but there's something magical about turning on the 3D layers and having students look around the building as though they were there. (Trust me, you can get a lot closer to the White House in Google Earth than you'll ever get on the public tour!)

Project Idea: Have Students Create a 3D Model Using Google SketchUp

I mentioned earlier that 3D models exist due to contributions from Google engineers, as well as user creations from around the world. So, just how do people make the models? A few years ago, Google released Google SketchUp, a free three-dimensional drafting program. Google SketchUp is a fantastic program that allows students to make their own models of buildings from around the world.

A popular activity in secondary schools is to have students create models of local buildings or attractions they're studying. Imagine having your students create models of your school building or the town hall. To view a collection of student-created models, look at the K–12 Education Google SketchUp Gallery at http://picasaweb.google.com/gallery.sketchup/Education K12#. For information about creating the models and uploading them to Google Earth, go to http://sketchup.google.com/training/videos/gsuge.html. Creating 3D models of your world is a great example of real-world projects for students using Google Earth and Google SketchUp.

> **NETS-S Standard I Objective c**
>
> Students demonstrate creative thinking, construct knowledge, and develop innovative products and processes using technology. Students use models and simulations to explore complex systems and issues. (ISTE, 2007)

Street View is another Google Earth innovation. One of the minor complaints in the early days of Google Earth was that aerial photos could only provide users with one angle of the world. Seeing places from above was helpful, but we wanted more. People wanted to experience what areas would look like from the ground. The Google Earth team responded. Starting in 2007, maps became three dimensional as Google staff traveled the globe to take pictures of places from the street view. Now you could see locations in Google Earth just as you would if you were standing in the actual spot. It gave users a sense of realism that was difficult to achieve otherwise. Before Street View, teachers could have students travel to locations and look down on the areas; now activities could actually take place at the locations.

Street View not only allows you to look at a location, but you can actually travel along the streets and pan around to see everything that's around you (see Figure 8.8).

- To move up and down the street, click the arrows on the road. This will change the photos to simulate movement.
- To "look around" on the street, use your mouse and click on the area of the photo you wish to view up close. Google will shift your perspective and give you a 360° view of the area.

Figure 8.8 Looking Around in Street View

Earlier, I shared the idea of having kids trace their walking route to school using directions. Now, combine that with Street View, and you can actually have kids take an exact path between home and school. The students can pan around the screen and see places they are familiar with. For younger children, the line between virtual and reality is nearly nonexistent.

Google Earth provides some of the most realistic photos you'll find depicting various locations around the world. To enhance the aerial photos in the program, try turning on the **Photos** layer. In this layer, you'll encounter user-submitted photos from Panoramio, a partner site with Google Earth (see Figure 8.9). Photos allows you to see places in the world through the eyes of people who've been there before. Let's say your students are using Google Earth to explore Mount Rushmore. You want to look around the monument, so you turn on the 3D Buildings layer; the problem is that the model doesn't really provide you with a great view of the huge sculpture.

Now you turn on the Photos layer and instantly, dozens of tiny blue squares appear on the map. As you click on each of the icons, an image appears showing you various aspects of the incredible edifice. Your students can see, first hand, several different angles showing the monument. Each of these images was provided by someone who had traveled to Mount Rushmore and shared their experience class by uploading their photos to the website, Panoramio (see Figure 8.9).

Figure 8.9   Panoramio Layer Provides Photos

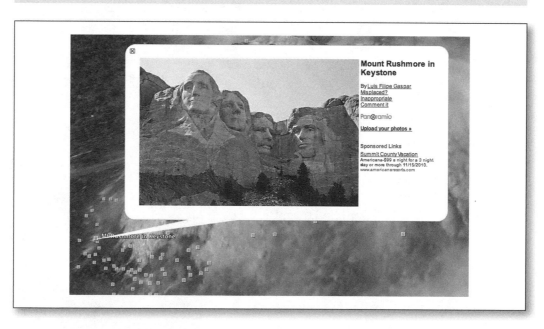

The Photos layer isn't the only place where you can find quality images in Google Earth. There are actually three other layers containing high-resolution images of various locations, Gigapan/Gigapixl photos and Cities 360. All of these collections are found within the Gallery folder.

Gigipan/Gigapixl and **Cities 360** use panoramic photos to show details of landmarks and locations that you can't find in your average photo. Take a trip to China, and you'll certainly want to visit the Forbidden City. With the Gigipan Photos layer on, your students can experience the same amazing architecture using an incredible image on the screen that you actually "fly into" to see up close. Using the scroll wheel on your mouse, you can get up close to various aspects of the photo. Since it is a high-resolution photo, the image won't blur or degrade as you zoom in (see Figure 8.10).

Figure 8.10 High-Resolution Photos in Gigapan Layer

The **YouTube** layer provides another first-person view of the world, through video. As with other layers we've discussed in this section, turning on the YouTube layer provides users with visual material submitted by people across the globe. You'll find everything from videos of a tourist's first trip to Disney World to a base jumper's flight from the fingers of Christ the Redeemer in Rio de Janeiro, Brazil. It's an amazing way to see the world in a new light.

USING REAL-TIME DATA WITH WEATHER, ■ OCEANS, AND SUNRISE/SUNSET

Because Google Earth utilizes a high-speed Internet connection, it has the power to access *real-time data* in ways that other information sources cannot.

> It may be cliché to emphasize the world wide aspect of the Web, but Internet technologies have lowered the proverbial walls of the class-room, giving students access to information that far surpasses the print-bound copies of encyclopedias and periodicals that were once the standard for K–12 research projects. (Watters, 2010, n.p.)

Take the Weather and Oceans layers in Google Earth. Each of these layers ties into international databases of information to provide users with real-time information on a variety of science-related topics. Over the course of a lesson, students, using the Weather layer, can actually see evidence of how temperature or radar patterns have changed in a given location.

Weather

Even though this layer isn't new to Google Earth, it keeps changing and adding new features. In the latest version (Version 6) of Google Earth, the Weather layer "projects images of rain and snow over the areas with those weather patterns as it's actually happening" (Melanson, 2010, n.p.).

Can you imagine looking at your area in Google Earth, noticing that it's snowing in the Weather layer, and then having your elementary students look out the nearest window to confirm the current weather (see Figure 8.11)? Think of having your secondary school students track a tropical storm as it is moving across the ocean toward land. The Weather layer provides students with basic tools to help them identify weather patterns and make predictions. This is using real-time data at its best!

| Figure 8.11 | Watch Snow Fall in Google Earth |

Having students explore weather patterns is a great way to have them explore information on deeper levels. The kids can make predictions, evaluate patterns, and identify changes—all by watching temperature and radar patterns in Google Earth.

| Figure 8.12 | The Oceans Layer |

Oceans

This layer is still relatively new in Google Earth, but it didn't take long for its impact to be noticed. Using the Oceans layer, you'll find information from tons of different sources. There's everything from videos by the Cousteau Ocean World to historical information about ancient and modern shipwrecks. You can even learn about endangered species using several different layers.

One of the best ways to have students explore the oceans in an innovative way is by turning on the **Animal Tracking** layer found inside of the

Oceans layer. Here, you'll be able to swim along with dolphins, sharks, and whales as they cruise through the world's oceans. Hundreds of marine animals have been tagged with tracking devices, allowing us to observe their travel patterns and understand much of their movement beneath the water. As you follow different animals, you can actually turn on time-lapse animations to see their travels up close. What a great way to learn about marine biology!

Sunrise/Sunset

This isn't really a layer; rather, it's a tool that allows the user to access real-time data to chart the earth's orbit and rotations by checking the sunrise and sunset. Located on the toolbar across the top of the map, the Sunrise/Sunset option provides users with the ability to watch the sun rise and set in a given location.

Using the Sunrise/Sunset tool is a great way to teach younger students about the differences between night and day (see Figure 8.13). Here's how it works:

1. Find the toolbar across the top of your map in Google Earth.

2. Turn on the tool by clicking on the image of a sunrise.

3. Use the Time slider to see how the sun travels across the world turning day into night and back again.

Figure 8.13   Track the Sun Using Sunrise/Sunset

Source: © 2011 INEGI.

The kids will see how the sky gets lighter as the sun rises in that area. As you zoom in to a city and change your perspective from overhead to across the horizon, you'll actually see the sun rise in the east and set in the west.

With older students, you can use the Sunrise/Sunset feature to have students make predictions about the way in which the time of year impacts the sunrise and sunset and the length of the day. It's another interesting way to have kids interpret real-time data to make conclusions about the world.

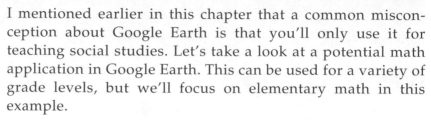

Project Idea: Measuring the World Around You

NETS-S Standard 3 Objective b

Students apply digital tools to gather, evaluate, and use information. Students locate, organize, analyze, evaluate, synthesize, and ethically use information from a variety of sources and media. (ISTE, 2007)

I mentioned earlier in this chapter that a common misconception about Google Earth is that you'll only use it for teaching social studies. Let's take a look at a potential math application in Google Earth. This can be used for a variety of grade levels, but we'll focus on elementary math in this example.

One of my favorite tools along the top toolbar of Google Earth is the **Measurement** tool (see Figure 8.14). The icon for this tool is a blue ruler, inconspicuous enough that you might overlook it if you're not paying attention. Here's how it works.

The Measurement tool has two options:

1. Line: measures the distance between two points
2. Path: measures distances between more than two points.

Figure 8.14 Use the Measurement Tool for Math

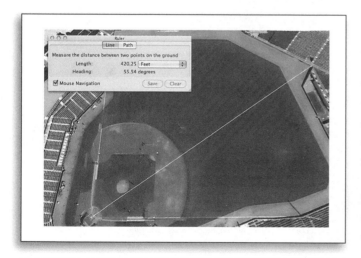

Source: © 2011 INEGI.

Here's an example of using the line tool that involves using estimation and then gathering data to test that estimate. If I want my students to understand distances and units of measurement, I could give them some standard story problem from a math textbook. Or, using Google Earth, I could take the students to Fenway Park in Boston and have them estimate the distance of a home run to dead centerfield. Which do you think would be more engaging for fifth-graders?

Using the Measurement tool in the **line** mode, students can mark home plate and drag a line out to centerfield to discover the distance a home run actually travels.

We can extend this lesson by exploring different units of measurement as well. In the Measurement tool, there's a drop-down menu that provides options to display the distance in feet, miles, meters, and more. For our home run example, we wouldn't want to leave the distance in miles; rather, the kids will want to switch the unit of measurement to feet. It's a great way to help kids understand the relationship between various units of measurement in a real-world example they can relate to.

If I switch to the **path** mode of the measurement tool, we can find the perimeter or any building or monument. Imagine using Google Earth to have the kids measure the distance around the school or have them discover just how big the Grand Canyon actually is.

Project Idea: Google Lit Trips for Language Arts

One of the most innovative ways to use Google Earth as a teaching tool is the creation of a multimedia virtual tour called a Google Lit Trip. When you think about most books we assign our students, the major criticism teachers hear is, how does this relate to the real world? With Google Earth, you can take your students to the actual places they are reading about in a story and engage them with questions and activities (see Figure 8.15).

> **NETS-S Standard 1 Objective a**
>
> Students demonstrate creative thinking, construct knowledge, and develop innovative products and processes using technology. Students apply existing knowledge to generate new ideas, products, or processes. (ISTE, 2007)

The basic idea of a Lit Trip is that you create location markers about different elements of a book. Each marker contains a combination of text and various multimedia elements to provide the users with a virtual fieldtrip related to a book they are reading. Once the tours are compiled, students can literally fly to various parts of the books and experience the sites firsthand. Take a look at a fantastic collection of Lit Trips at www.googlelittrips.com. There, you'll find dozens of trips organized for a variety of grade levels. They range from kindergarten all the way through higher education. Googlelittrips.com is an incredible resource for teachers looking to create virtual tours with their own students.

Figure 8.15 Google Lit Trip Example

Figure 8.16 Change Placemark Name and Add Description

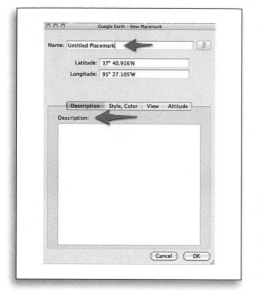

For example, a kindergarten class can take a tour of the Boston Harbor with the teacher as they explore the different locations found in *Make Way for Ducklings.* Each of the locations in the book is brought to life through text and images that encourage students to think about issues in the book and visualize the events they read. Check out the tour online at http://googlelittrips.com/GoogleLit/K-5/Entries/2007/11/16_Make_Way_for_Ducklings_by_Robert_McCloskey.html

Lit Trips are a great activity for all ages of student; the older students (Grades 3–12) can create their own Lit Trips, and the younger kids can travel along a tour made by their teacher. The Lit Trip assignment is highly engaging for students, as it encourages them to explore the world through the places they've learned about in class. As we learn from West Yellowstone School librarian and technology teacher Jo Stevens, some students can't get enough of working on the interactive tours: "The students' work ethic was incredible. Some students even came in before and after school [to work on their projects]," Stevens said (as quoted in Tumbleson, 2011, n.p.).

Creating a Google Lit Trip

- Search for a location from the book you'll be reading with your class. Using the basic search function in Google Earth, type in the first location from your text. Once you navigate to the proper destination, it's time to mark the location.

- Create a *Placemark* for your location. The Placemark tool is located along the top left corner of your Google Earth map. The icon is a yellow pushpin that marks the latitude and longitude of your current location. Once you drop a placemark on the screen, you'll find that a description window opens, allowing you to add the content for your virtual tour (see Figure 8.16).

- Add and edit text in your placemarks. With the description window open for your placemark, you're ready to customize the marker with details from the book. By default, all placemarks start as Untitled Placemark. Start by naming the placemark with an event from the book. For example, if the location depicts the scene where the animals overtake the farmhouse in *Animal Farm*, "Animal Revolution" may be an appropriate title for the placemark.

After naming the placemark, it's time to add text to the Description field. The **Description** field is an HTML-formatted text box, so you may type whatever you choose and arrange the content using HTML. The type of text is up to you, but a traditional Lit Trip includes a couple of basic elements.

1. Summary of the event from the book. Usually, it's not more than a paragraph and may include a quotation or reference from the book.

For example, from the book *Hatchet*, by Gary Paulson, I would use a summary of a chapter in the book to introduce some guiding questions: *Brian encounters a moose, a female with no horns, who drives him into the lake. She is relentless in her attack, and Brian quickly realizes how hurt he is. He thinks the moose has broken his ribs.*

2. Discussion questions or activity. Another component of most Lit Trips is an activity prompt or discussion questions. Use these as a way to help guide the students' comprehension of the book by engaging them with various prompts. Again, from *Hatchet*,

What do you think will happen next to Brian?
How would you try to start a fire without matches?

Combining Google Earth with literature study allows teachers to come up with activities that are highly creative for their students. Instead of having students use this powerful tool just to make a plot summary, Jerome Burg, English teacher and technology-integration coordinator, suggests nudging them toward activities that will generate higher-order questions and more analytical thinking (Boss, n.d.-a).

I mentioned that the Description field can be formatted using HTML. You may notice that, when viewed, the placemark text all combines into one large paragraph. All of the spacing you provided doesn't seem to be working. This is because you need to format items like line spacing using HTML.

There are lots of different ways to format with HTML, but let's keep this simple.

- o If you want a single space between your text, use the <br> tag. This means type <br> in between two lines of text and you'll create a line break.
- o If you want things double-spaced, use the <p> tag. It should look something like this example from *Hatchet*:

After all he's gone through, Brian realizes the beauty that surrounds him. He takes a moment to reflect upon how lucky he is to have survived the crash.

<p>

Discussion:<p>

*1. Share a time in your life when you've realized something important.
*

2. Why do you feel Brian's attitude is changing?

Using a few basic HTML tags will help you format the text the way you want. It will make it easier to read for the students, and as an added bonus, you just learned a little web design. Pretty cool, huh?!

- • Add an image to your Lit Trip. One of the creative aspects of the Lit Trip is the ability to add multimedia to the placemarks. It gives the real-world location a tie-in with the book and makes the tour much more engaging.

So what types of images are used in a Lit Trip? Generally, the idea is to use images that illustrate the events from the book. You can use images directly from the book, such as if it's a children's book. The images could be digital photos that students took themselves. They can be images that students find on the web. The key to having an image displayed in the placemark is that the image has to exist online or in a digital format already.

To get your images in a digital format, you'll need to use a digital camera or a scanner. If you want to use images directly from the children's book, you can either scan the pages or take digital photos of the pages. Once you have digital images, you will need to get them online so they'll display in Google Earth. There are several ways to get your digital images online. Since we're focusing on Google tools in this book, let's explore how you store your photos online using your Google account.

Google provides you with 1 GB of online storage for your digital images. As mentioned earlier, it's called the Picasa Web Album, and it's free! Here's how to find the Web Album.

1. Go to http://picasaweb.google.com. After you sign in to the Web Album, you'll land on the Home tab. If this is your first time here, there won't be any content. If you're using other Google tools (like Blogger or Google+), you may find that some albums of images already exist, as this is the default image storage for Google.

↑ Upload

2. To add your photos to the library, click on the **Upload** button.

3. You'll be asked if you want to Add the photos to an existing album or if you want to Create a new album. Choose **Create a new album.**

4. Name the album based upon the title of the book you're using for the Lit Trip.

Uploading Images to the Web Album

After you've set up the album structure, now you're ready to upload the images. You can upload up to five images at a time into the album. Uploading the image is much like attaching a document to an e-mail. Here are the steps:

1. Click the **Choose File** button.

2. You'll be prompted to browse your computer to find the images you'd like to use.

3. Select up to five for upload at a time.

4. Click on the **Start Upload** button, and a few moments later, the images will be online in your Web Album.

Adding the Image to Your Lit Trip

With your photos in the online Web Album, you can now add the images to your Google Lit Trip. Each image has its own unique web address. This is necessary for the image to display properly (see Figure 8.17).

- To access the address for the image, right click on the desired photo.
- Select the **Copy Image URL** or the **Copy Image Address** link in the menu (see Figure 8.17). Selecting this option copies the image's web address or URL to the clipboard so it can be pasted into Google Earth.

Figure 8.17 Copying the Image's Web Address

Used with permission of Jared Covili.

Let's get the image into our placemark back in Google Earth. This will require us to learn another HTML code. The image tag, or <img>, helps our pictures to show up in Google Earth. Images won't display properly unless we use this simple tag.

Just like before, we need to use the < and > symbols to indicate we're creating an HTML tag. Here's what the tag looks like for inserting an image using HTML.

```
<img src="https://lh5.googleusercontent.com/_UrSpde3V5ZY/TUib2G1UNEI/AAAAAAA
AG_U/1W-Jun7C6u0/s640/DSCN0639.JPG">
```

Now, I know this looks a little daunting, but let's break it down. Let's start with <img src=" https://lh5.googleusercontent.com/_UrSpde3V5ZY/TUib2 G1UNEI/AAAAAAAG_U/1W-Jun7C6u0/s640/DSCN0639.JPG">

- img stands for image.
- src refers to the source of the image, meaning the source of the image online.
- After that, you're simply indicating where the image resides online by pasting in the copied URL.

The example above indicates the URL for the image I used. Your URL will be slightly different, but it should include the website address, followed by the path to the specific images. An image file usually ends with the .jpg file extension. When you put all the pieces together, you're using HTML to bring the image off the Internet and insert it into the placemark.

There are a few things to note about inserting the image using HTML:

1. It doesn't matter if the text is capitalized or not.

2. The spelling *does* matter. If there are any typos, the image won't display.

3. There must be a space between img and src.

4. You need to use quotation marks surrounding the image URL.

5. When you paste the image URL, it should end with an image file extension such as jpg, gif, and so forth.

Once the HTML is inserted into the placemark, you should see the image display properly.

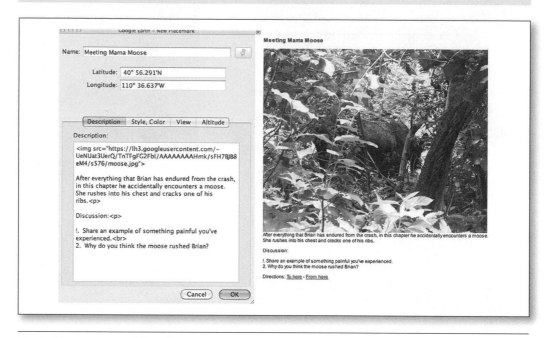

Figure 8.18 HTML and Display View of Placemark

Used with permission of Google Inc. and Lauretta Williams.

Now your placemark is ready to display both image and text (see Figure 8.18). Let's test it out. When you click on the placemark, Google Earth will zoom into the marked location on the map, and the contents of the placemark will display on the screen.

After creating one placemark, just repeat the process as you create markers for other events from the book you're interested in highlighting. If you choose to, you can implement other multimedia elements like video. As with inserting an image, you'll need the HTML code for these items.

> *Version 6.2.0.5905 now includes an Add Image button. This button actually builds the HTML code for you! You still need the URL for the image, but using the Add Image button eliminates the need to type HTML code.*

Embedding Video in Your Lit Trip

To incorporate YouTube video clips into your Lit Trip, do the following:

1. Go to youtube.com.

2. Find your desired video.

3. At the bottom of each video in YouTube, find the **Share** button.

4. You want to use the **Embed** option.

5. Check the box for old embed code at the bottom of the list of options.

6. Just copy that code and paste it into your placemark. As long as the video remains on YouTube, you'll see it in your Lit Trip (see Figure 8.19).

Figure 8.19   Embed Code for YouTube Video

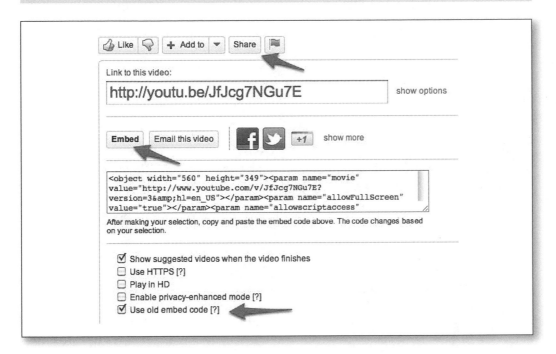

There are other options for customizing your placemarks using HTML code. I'd suggest checking the Google Lit Trip website (www.googlelittrips .com) for tons of examples. If you're not sure about how to type the necessary HTML code, you'll find dozens of websites that provide examples. A simple Google search for HTML code should move you in the right direction.

Taking the Tour on the Road

Once you create all the placemarks you want to use in your Lit Trip, it's time to package the entire tour together into a file you can share with others (see Figure 8.20). Up to now, all the placemarks should be located in the Places section of Google Earth. Each has a separate icon and its own location on the map. We need to group all the placemarks together so they can be saved in one file.

Creating and Using a Folder for Your Tour

The key to packaging the placemarks is to make a folder. This container will house all the placemarks in one location. Creating a folder is simple.

1. Click on the **Add** menu and select the **folder** option.

2. Name the folder and provide a description of the project.

3. Choose **Save** to protect your work.

Figure 8.20   Packaging Your Google Lit Trip in a Folder

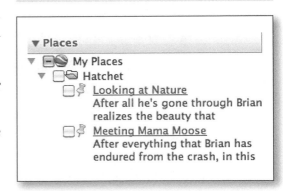

4. The new folder should be in the Places area, near the placemarks. It may help to drag the folder to the top of the Places tab, with all the placemarks beneath it.

5. To add the placemarks, drag and drop each into the folder. Once a placemark is inside the folder, the icon will be indented from the main folder. You can drag placemarks around inside the folder to determine the correct order for your tour. Most start with the first event and work their way through to the end.

6. Our last major step in packaging the lit trip is to save the tour. Saving the project as a KMZ file (one with a .kmz extension) allows us to create a portable version of our Lit Trip.

7. To save the project, right click on the folder and select **Save Project As** from the menu that appears.

You have successfully created a Google Lit Trip.

Now that your trip has been saved to the computer, it can be shared with others in any number of ways. E-mail it, post it to the web, even transfer the file with portable storage—it's up to you.

I know this example focuses on using Google Earth to create a Lit Trip, but these virtual tours can encompass any curriculum area. Whether you're exploring volcanoes from around the world, studying a real-world example of Fibonacci's sequence, or visiting the beaches of Normandy, Google Earth is the perfect tool to see these examples firsthand.

MORE IDEAS FOR GOING GOOGLE

Other Google Earth Project Ideas

- Use the **Historical Imagery** button to see the changes an area has made over time. This is a great way to see the history of an older school and the surrounding community. Some of the images go back several decades. It's amazing to see the growth in different parts of the world!

- Google Earth can help you explore the heavens, as well as the Earth. When you click on the **Google Sky** button, your perspective immediately shifts to outer space. You'll take your students on a journey around the solar system to study the planets, constellations, stars, and NASA space explorations. What an incredible way to teach your students various elements of astronomy during the daytime hours of school. Google Sky uses simulations and photography from a variety of NASA satellites to capture the universe we've only imagined until now.

  Not only can you explore the universe as a whole, but Google also provides users with in-depth information on both the Moon and Mars. You'll learn historical information from various lunar expeditions and view aspects of these celestial bodies from a totally new perspective. With image overlays and photos from the Hubble space telescope, you'll feel like you were with the astronauts on one of the Apollo missions.

- Have the students record their journeys around the world. Using the video camera button, students can create screen recordings of their trips to various locations. Plug in a microphone and the kids can actually provide their own narratives or unique travelogues to places around the globe. This is a great way for students to create personal reports about countries, states, or even cities. This file can be saved and shared for others to view as well.

TIPS FOR THE GOOGLE CLASSROOM

- The Layers panel can quickly overtake the screen if you leave all the various data fields turned on. When you move between different layers, be sure to "turn off" the ones you've finished using.
- As you create placemarks of locations on the map, check to make sure the placemarks don't end up in a temporary folder. All the data will be lost if the program crashes or you forget to save properly.
- When searching for a location, the search results will include a variety of advertisements for different companies near that location. You can remove all unwanted search results by selecting the **X** in the lower right corner of the search panel.
- To ensure you have the most recent version of Google Earth, click on the **Help** menu and select **Check for Updates Online**. Updated versions of Google Earth come out periodically, and it's important to have access to all the latest features.

9

Picasa and Picasa Web Album

--- ➰➰ ---

FIVE THINGS TO KNOW ABOUT PICASA

1. Picasa automatically organizes photos on your computer into folders.
2. Picasa has over 20 unique editing features.
3. Edits in Picasa are non-destructive; you will still have your original photos intact.
4. You can sync your photos from the computer to the Picasa Web Album.
5. You have 1 GB of free storage for your photos in the Picasa Web Album.

--- ➰➰ ---

When multimedia in the classroom comes up as a topic, a discussion of using digital images with students often ensues. Our kids all seem to have access to digital cameras (even if it's only on their cell phone), and they love taking pictures of the world around them. Says Dan Mayer, a teacher at San Lorenzo Valley High School, near Santa Cruz, California,

> It was like a dam broke. Before that, I didn't think about finding visuals for the classroom. . . . Now, I'm walking around daily, thinking about it. I walk around with a digital camera on my phone. As I become more acquainted with my subject matter and more enthusiastic about it, I see examples of it everywhere. And the examples are 100 percent of the time better than what my textbook would have me use to introduce a topic. (as quoted in Boss, 2008, n.p.)

In the past decade, digital photo editing and multimedia project creation with these images has become an essential skill. It allows students the opportunity

115

to develop their creativity and see the world through their own lens. It's a skill that, once learned, will be with students throughout their entire education and follow them into the modern workforce. In a recent study sponsored by Adobe, the researchers discovered the role that a creative mind plays in a productive work environment.

> Creativity, in fact, is now becoming a sought-after skill in all walks of life. According to a survey, Creativity in the Classroom, by digital media specialist Adobe, some 77% of employers and higher education lecturers quizzed said that they viewed "creativity"—interpreted as the ability to generate ideas, developing online content, delivering persuasive, polished presentations or being imaginative problem-solvers—as "an essential or important skill," alongside the basic ones of literacy and numeracy. (Nightingale, 2011, n.p.)

■ GETTING STARTED WITH PICASA

As with Google Earth, Picasa has both a downloadable program and an online service. In this section, we'll explore how you can organize, edit, and create unique projects using digital images in the download program of Picasa. We'll also demonstrate how you can share and store photos online using the Picasa Web Album site. While the tools have different purposes, they really work together to help users work with their digital photos. In order to simplify and clarify our discussion, we'll refer to the downloaded program as Picasa and the online tool as the Picasa Web Album.

- Find Picasa at http://picasa.google.com. It's a free download, but you'll need to ensure your computer meets the minimum requirements. Picasa works on both the Mac and Windows operating systems.
- Picasa will request permission to search your computer for images. You'll have two options: Search the entire computer or search in some primary folders (Desktop, My Pictures, and My Documents). If you're on your own computer or your primary school computer, I'd suggest searching the entire computer for images.
- Picasa will find all the images and make a virtual catalog within its program library. Imagine if you hired someone to come to your house and organize your boxes of old photos. In essence, that's exactly what Picasa's doing for you. It will find all your photos and organize them by date in its library.

Picasa finds all the images, but it doesn't make duplicate copies of the pictures for its program. Rather, Picasa creates a *virtual* copy of the images. That means your computer's storage doesn't fill up with a bunch of the same images. Picasa simply references the original image and allows you to make edits to the virtual copy. The original image remains intact. Any edits made to the image exist only with the virtual copy within Picasa.

Picasa Basics

Importing

There are a couple of basic ways to add or "import" your photos to the Picasa library. The first is to import them from a digital camera.

- Connect your digital camera to your computer (or insert your memory card in your printer, if it has a photo transfer function). A window should come up on the screen prompts you to transfer the photos to the computer. Now, depending on whether you're on a PC or Mac, you'll have a couple of options.

  o On a PC, you should see a menu display with choices for transferring the images. One of the choices should be to Copy Pictures to the Computer Using Picasa. This is the simplest way to move the images from camera to computer.

  o On a Mac, you may have to choose between downloading the pictures with iPhoto or Picasa. By default, most Mac computers use iPhoto for image transfer, and that's okay. You can give Picasa access to the iPhoto library, and you'll immediately find all of your pictures.

  o Note that when you add images to Picasa from your camera, Picasa will want to import the images to the computer's default image folder (This is usually the Pictures folder.). You'll need to select a different folder if you would rather they were stored somewhere else.

- The second option for adding images to Picasa is to use the Import button.

  o Located in the top left corner of the Picasa interface, the **Import** button will prompt you to browse folders to find images and add them to your Picasa library.

  o When you select the Import button, a new tab will open up along the top of the Picasa interface. Here, you'll need to choose which photos you'd like to add to your library.

  o When you browse to a particular folder, Picasa will display all the images inside. You can select all the pictures or choose only those you'd like to add. Picasa will let you know if you're trying to add photos that already exist in the library by putting a duplicate symbol on the pictures.

Once you're using Picasa, you can have the program keep track of new photos added to the computer directly. Located in the tools menu, select the **Folder Manager** option. You can tell Picasa which folder to check automatically for new images. After enabling the Folder Options, relax—and let Picasa do the rest.

Organizing

One of the biggest challenges most teachers face with using digital images is file management. Over the years, photos have been added to the computer, but now it's hard to find all those images. Understanding how you

Figure 9.1 Picasa Organizes Your Photos in Folders

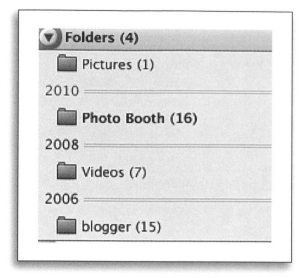

can organize and find your pictures will make a big difference in your ability to use the photos in classroom projects.

While it's finding all the images Picasa is organizing the photos chronologically into folders (see Figure 9.1). All images have date stamps embedded into the photo's file data. Picasa simply reads those dates and organizes the folders from newest to oldest. You'll find the folders placed into groups by year. Photos taken in 2009 will be categorized together, as will any images from previous years.

Now it's important to remember that Picasa will use the oldest photo in a given folder to determine its year in the library. So, if I take a bunch of pictures in 2011 and copy some images from 2007 into the same folder, Picasa will organize that folder under 2007 for its library.

Let's learn a few more things about folders in Picasa:

- When you select any of the folders in the library, Picasa will immediately display all the photos from that folder in thumbnail format.
- Rearranging the images in a folder is easy with Picasa. Just left click on the photo and drag it to your desired location.
- You can also move images from one folder to another in Picasa. Drag an entire folder of images onto another folder, and you'll be prompted to merge the two folders together.
- Deleting an image in Picasa will result in the image being deleted from the computer entirely. The same is true with folders; if you delete a folder in Picasa, it deletes the folder from the computer. Earlier, I mentioned that Picasa's edits are non-destructive, but it's important to note that Picasa is referencing the original image on the hard drive. *Deleting an image in Picasa means you are removing the image from the hard drive.*

Figure 9.2 People, Places, and Tags in Picasa

Using People, Places, and Tags When you organize your hard copy prints at home, there are a few common categories. Generally, we want to write down who is in the pictures, where the pictures were taken, and what event the pictures depict. Picasa has a great system to help you organize online for these basic categories. Located in the bottom right corner of the program, People, Places, and Tags can help you find your images and sort them (see Figure 9.2).

When you select the **People** option, Picasa screens the selected folder of photos for individual faces. Click on a photo, and you'll find that the faces are indentified in the image with a box (see Figure 9.3). Now, the first time a person appears in People, the computer won't be able to recognize him or her, so you'll have to establish the person by typing in the person's name tag. Once named, though, Picasa will identify other photos in which the person appears. It takes confirming a few photos to help train the program, but you will soon see that Picasa will find new photos of a person and add them to the group.

After you start finding and naming people in Picasa, a new library item for People will appear along the top left side of the screen. Here, you'll find all of the people you've named, along with an **Unnamed people** category for those you haven't identified.

Using the People option can dramatically speed up your ability to find images of a specific student. People can help you create projects or assessments for one of your students or use it simply to help learn students' names at the beginning of the school year.

The **Places** option allows you to create a unique map of the world with your digital photos. You can select each photo individually or add an entire folder of images at once.

To add an image placemark to the map,

Figure 9.3 Selecting a Face in People

Used with permission of Google Inc., and Jared Covili.

1. Choose an image or folder of images.
2. Select the **Places** marker.
3. Type in the address of the desired location. Places utilizes the data from Google Maps. The more specific you are with the address, the better results you'll receive.

4. The map will zoom in to the requested location.
5. To add markers to the map, double click on the **Placemark** icon next to the zoom slider (see Figure 9.4). Your cursor will attach to the icon, and you'll be able to drag the symbol down to your map. Click on the map once the placemark is in the right spot on the map.

Figure 9.4 Add a Placemark to the Map in Places

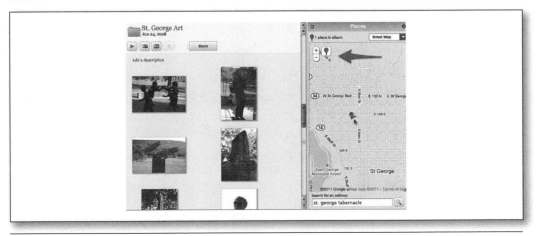

Used with permission of Google Inc., and Jared Covili.

After using Places you'll never need to ask, "Now, where was that photo taken again?"

The **Tags** tool enables you to label images based upon a common characteristic. When you apply tags to a group of photos, it marks them with a keyword. Say, for example, you want to mark all the pictures from the school's Halloween parade. Using tags, you'd simply apply the keyword (or tag) "Halloween Parade" to those selected images.

Once a keyword is created, it's easy to apply it to other images. Simply select the photo or folder of images and click on the tag icon in the lower right corner of the screen. As with the other management tools, the Tag tool opens up a panel along the right side of the screen. You'll need to set up a new tag by typing a keyword in the open area and hitting the + sign. This will create the tag and place it in the keyword bin at the bottom of the panel. Apply the tag by selecting an image, choosing the tab, and hitting the + sign. You can assign multiple tags to the same image or group of pictures (see Figure 9.5).

Figure 9.5 Applying Tags in Picasa

Used with permission of Google Inc., and Jared Covili.

The best feature in Tags is that they help you locate your photos, as tags are searchable. In the top right corner of Picasa, you'll find a search box. When you type in the name of a tag, Picasa immediately sorts through all your photos and produces a filtered group of photos using that tag.

Creating and Using Albums   **Albums** allow you to create a folder in which you store similar images. They can be from one event, a given time frame, or a particular topic. For classroom use, you can create an album that follows a specific curriculum topic, e.g., images depicting symmetry, or photos for a science lesson on plants.

1. To create an album, select a photo or group of photos. When images are selected, a thumbnail of the photo displays in the Selection Tray located in the bottom right corner of the program.

2. Choose the **Album** icon found to the right of the Selection Tray.

3. Create a new album, or select from existing albums. You can add one photo at a time, or choose a collection of photos and add them all at once.

4. Once an album has been created, you can also add photos by right clicking on them and selecting the **Add to Album** option.

Starred Photos   Another quick option for selecting your favorite images is the **Starred photo** tag. Found near the bottom left corner of Picasa, this tool allows you to add a star to your best pictures.

1. To add a star to a photo, select the images(s) and click on the **Starred photo** icon.

2. You'll find that a tiny star will appear on the photos in the bottom left corner of each.

3. Once a star has been applied to a photo, you can perform a targeted search for the starred photos using the **Filters** menu along the top of the screen. All starred photos will appear in the library.

4. If you choose to remove the star from an image, just select the image and click on the **Starred photo** symbol again. This clears the symbol from the picture.

Now that you've seen how Picasa helps you to organize your photos, let's explore how you can edit your pictures and prepare them for future classroom projects.

Editing With Picasa

Picasa provides you with tons of basic and creative editing options. Many programs allow you to correct red eye and crop an image, but very few contain the variety of editing controls found in Picasa.

- To begin editing images in Picasa, double click on a photo in your library. You'll discover that all the menus have changed. Instead of seeing the folder structure found in the organize mode, now the left side of the screen displays various editing controls. Rather than looking at thumbnails of your images, you can select only one image at a time to work on.
- Picasa has three different areas of editing for you to implement: Basic fixes, Tuning, and Effects.

Figure 9.6   Basic Fixes in Picasa

- It's important to note that edits made within Picasa are stored on the virtual copy of your images. This means your original photos remain unaltered on your computer. All of the edits made within Picasa are considered non-destructive.

Basic Fixes

In Picasa's latest update for the PC, the Picnik tool is incorporated as two new editing tabs rather than as a tool in Basic Fixes. Also, the editing tabs now have icons rather than text.

Picasa offers several basic fixes to help you correct common problems found in many photos (see Figure 9.6). There's everything from tools to help you compose a good image, to color and light correction, and even a blemish remover. Picasa's free tools are certainly a highlight of this program.

The **Crop** tool allows you to recompose your images. Many times, we take photos that need a slightly different perspective to add depth to the image or remove unwanted extras from the picture.

To crop an image,

1. Select the **Crop** button from **Basic Fixes.**

2. Picasa provides you with three choices of preset crop options. Choose a photo from the thumbnail images, or use the drop-down menu to choose from a variety of print sizes.

3. To manually set a crop area, click and drag a selection onto your image. As you create a crop selection, the image will display the selected area with a gray film. Once you create the selection, you can alter it by adjusting the dimensions through clicking and dragging on the perimeter handles. You can also move the crop selection around the image by clicking inside the selection and dragging it to a new location in the image.

4. Once you've settled on your selection, enact the crop by using the **Apply** button along the bottom right of the crop tools.

The **Red Eye** tool solves the most common issue we have with our photos of people. Red eye is a huge annoyance, but it's an easy fix in Picasa (see Figure 9.7). When you select a photo with red eye issues, just click on the **Red Eye** button in **Basic Fixes,** and watch what happens next. Picasa automatically identifies the problem area and replaces the red with a dark hue to fill in the pupil. Just like that, you're done!

Have you ever heard of a better name for a tool than **I'm Feeling Lucky?** With this tool, Picasa is suggesting you give them a chance to fix the picture in a purely auto mode. When using this button, Picasa will do a combination of fixes on both color and light, using a basic formula to enhance the image. This is a great tool to use on an image when you first start editing. Try it and see what happens.

Imagine having the ability to take minor blemishes and imperfections out of an otherwise fantastic photo. With the **Retouch** tool, Picasa gives you the ability to cover up an unwanted spot on an image (see Figure 9.8). This is a great

Figure 9.7 Fixing Red Eye With the Click of a Button

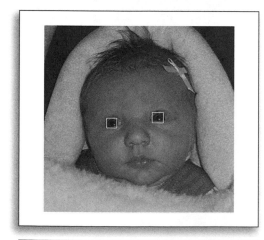

Used with permission of Google Inc., and Jared Covili.

tool for touching up a class or club photo, just enough to help students look their best in a group shot or closeup.

To touch up a photo,

1. Select the **Retouch** tool.

2. Your cursor will turn into a circular selection tool. Adjust the size of the tool using the brush size slider in the properties area.

3. Click on the blemish or damaged area. This will select those pixels for correction.

4. Click on an undamaged area of the photo that matches the texture of the problem selection.

5. Presto! Picasa automatically samples the clean area and covers up the blemish.

Figure 9.8   Retouching a Photo

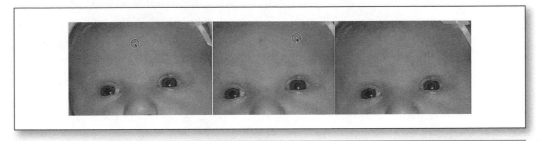

Used with permission of Google Inc., and Jared Covili.

The **Text** tool allows you to add titles and captions to your photos. This is a basic fix that can transform your images into teaching tools. Adding text can give emphasis to your pictures and provide students with the necessary information to understand deeper concepts. Further below, under Creating a Vocabulary Page, we'll look at adding and editing text in a project.

Tuning and Effects

Beyond using Basic Fixes, Picasa has two other editing areas to help you enhance your photos. The **Tuning** tab allows you to improve your images by correcting issues dealing with light and color. You can alter highlights, shadows, fill lights, and neutral colors using the sliders and buttons in this section of the Picasa editing tools.

The **Effects** tab has 12 different options to adjust your images and add emphasis to your subjects. Most of these effects are immediately applied to your image by clicking them. You can turn the photo to black and white or sepia with a single click. You can sharpen, warm, or add film grain as well.

Two of my favorite effects to make a subject come to life are **Focal B&W** and **Soft Focus.** Each of these tools relies on creating a new focal point in your image. Here's how they work:

1. After selecting your image, click on **Focal B&W** (see Figure 9.9).

2. Your image will go black and white, except for an area indicated by a green crosshair in the middle of the photo. This is your focal area, and it remains in color.

Figure 9.9 The Focal B&W Tool

3. To adjust your focal area, you'll find two different sliders in the tool properties along the left side of Picasa. You can adjust the size of the selection using that slider, or you can alter the sharpness of the selection with another slider.

The **Soft Focus** tool works in a similar manner, but the effect creates a focal point by blurring the parts of the image outside of the focal selection. Using these selection tools draws your students' attention immediately toward the focal area and provides you with a great place from which to begin instruction.

Project Idea: Creating a Vocabulary Page

NETS-S Standard 1 Objective a

Students demonstrate creative thinking, construct knowledge, and develop innovative products and processes using technology. Students apply existing knowledge to generate new ideas, products, or processes. (ISTE, 2007)

Adding text to an image can help you turn your photo into a fun vocabulary project. For this example, we'll create some first-year Spanish vocabulary. Here are the basic steps:

1. Open an image in Picasa and select the **Text** tool. You'll be prompted to type your desired text onto the image. Click anywhere on the picture, and type your vocabulary term. Let's add the Spanish term for Explorer, or *Explorar.*

2. Now that we've added our vocabulary term, Picasa gives us several different editing options for our text. To move the text, click and drag it to your chosen location. You can position your text vertically, horizontally, or diagonally. This means you can choose the best position for the text to help students understand the relationship between the text and the image.

3. To arrange text in a different position, move the mouse over the text. A box will appear that has a red dot along the right side. If you click and hold on the red dot, you can adjust your text in a variety of ways (see Figure 9.10. Also, you can increase the size of the font by clicking and dragging outward using the red dot.

4. After you've arranged your text, you may want to format it. You'll find several different choices for formatting your text in the tool's properties along the left side of the program. You can adjust the type of font, the color, outlining, transparency, and more.

Figure 9.10 Position Text Using the Red Dot

5. Once you finish making your adjustments, click the **Apply** button, and you're done. You've successfully added a vocabulary word to an image.

This is a fun project for students of any age. It allows the students the chance to learn new terms in a visual manner, which helps increase retention and understanding.

CREATE WITH PICASA ■

Picasa has several creative and innovative tools to help your students visualize concepts and share information. In the past, photos were printed and shared with the class, glued to a poster board or taped to a classroom wall. Once students viewed the images, they were basically forgotten. Picasa provides teachers and students with a wide array of project options to enhance learning and create lasting memories.

Project Idea: Creating a Collage

One of my favorite tools in Picasa is the **Collage** tool. This tool allows you to select a variety of photos and create different styles of collages. The layered photos can serve to show a topic in a combination of shared images. It is a great way to focus on a subject using several photos to illustrate parts of the concept.

> **NETS-S Standard 1 objective b**
>
> Students demonstrate creative thinking, construct knowledge, and develop innovative products and processes using technology. Students create original works as a means of personal or group expression. (ISTE, 2007)

1. Add the photos you want for the collage to the Selection Tray. If you click on a folder of images, all the pictures inside the folder are selected. There is no limit to the number of photos you can use, but the more images you select, the smaller they appear in the collage. To add images from multiple folders in Picasa, you'll need to choose pictures from one of the folders initially.

2. Once you've selected the photos from a given folder, you'll need to hold them in the Selection Tray. You accomplish this using the green pushpin icon located to the right of the Selection Tray. If you don't use the **Hold** button, when you pick photos from the second folder, it will clear all the images from the original selection.

Collage

3. Once you've got your images in the Selection Tray, it's time to click on the **Collage** button. This button is found along the bottom of the Picasa screen. There's also an option to make a collage in the **Create** menu across the top of the screen.

4. After clicking the Collage button, you'll see that a new tab has opened along the top of the screen. In the Collage tab, there are six different styles available to choose from. Each of the options has its strengths, but my personal favorites are the Mosaic and the Picture Pile.

   a. The **Mosaic** gives you the ability to arrange your photos in a tiled format. You can shuffle the images into a variety of patterns, so you can choose how your collage ends up. It's a great-looking project that you can use as part of a visual dictionary. Just pick several images of a subject, and you've got the foundation for a fun dictionary page.

   b. The **Picture Pile** takes the collage in an innovative new direction. Actually, it's an innovative *old* direction. The Picture Pile collage randomly "throws" your photos onto a canvas with a Polaroid-style border. You can a create class or club photo shoot that you could use in a yearbook or slideshow.

5. Once you've arranged your collage the way you like it, click on the **Create Collage** button to save a completed version of your compiled image. After creating the collage, a new folder will appear along the menu in your library. The Projects folder will be available, and you'll find any collages you've made inside.

To put a finishing touch on your collage, you'll want to use the **Text** tool to add a title to your project.

Project Idea: Creating a Movie

Another fantastic tool in Picasa is the ability to create a video using your stills and video clips. You can add music and titles to your project, creating a fun and simple way to share your images and clips as a movie.

1. As with the Collage tool, you'll need to select all the images and video you'd like to use in your project. All the same rules apply about choosing images from multiple folders.

2. Once you've selected all the contents for your project, click on the **Movie** button. It's located next to the Collage button, along the bottom tool bar in Picasa.

Movie

Just like we noticed with the Collage tool, a new tab has opened, and you're now ready to begin editing your video project. All the tools for the Movie tab will be located along the left side of Picasa.

By default, all of the clips are arranged in the same order they existed in the Selection Tray. You'll find the clips along the bottom of the Preview screen. You can move clips to a different location in the project by clicking and dragging the clip to a new spot in the timeline.

Editing Your Movie

There are three tabs of editing controls in the Movie Tool: Movie, Slide, and Clips.

On the **Movie** tab, you'll find controls to add music to your project, work with transitions, and alter the screen dimensions of the movie (see Figure 9.11). The **Slide** tab provides you with choices for adding and positioning text on your images and slides. The **Clips** tab allows you to bring additional images and video into your project.

Figure 9.11 Editing Controls in the Movie Tool

On any of the tabs, you have access to three publishing options for your video. You can close your project, send the video to YouTube, and/or create a copy of the movie.

Using the Movie Tab

There are two key elements for your project on the Movie tab, music and transition options or styles. When you click the **Load Music** option, you'll be prompted to browse your computer for a song. You can choose from a variety of music file types, including m4a, mp3, wav, and more.

Audio Options

- When you load a song, it includes the entire track. You don't have the option to edit down the song to a particular part of the track.
- Once you've added a song to the movie, you have a couple of controls over how the track plays. You can pick from the following options: Fit photos into audio, Truncate audio, or Loop photos to match audio.
- Depending on the length of the song, you may need to try some of the different options (e.g., if you have a long song, you might need to truncate the audio or loop the audio, unless you don't mind having the pictures on the screen for a long time).
- If you want to choose a different song, click on the **Clear** button and start the process again.

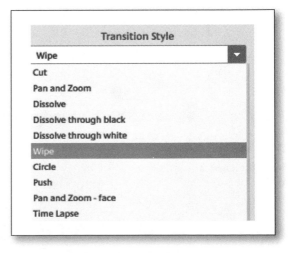

Figure 9.12 Ten Different Choices in the Transition Styles

Transition Options Within **Transition Style,** you'll find 10 different options for creating transitions between photos, such as wipe, dissolve, pan, and zoom (see Figure 9.12). One issue you'll encounter with the different transitions is you can only choose one style for the entire movie. You can't have some slides with a wipe transition and others utilizing the pan or zoom.

Using the Slide Tab

Adding titles to your movie can provide a polished feel to your project. By using the **Slide** tab, you can add text to the photos in your movie, create new title slides, and edit existing titles.

You may have noticed that Picasa created a default title for the movie by using the name of the main folder from which you selected photos. Most of the time, the name of the folder works fine for managing the images, but it doesn't always make for a great movie title.

To edit the title slide,

- You can change the font's attributes—i.e., font face, size, and style. You'll also be able to change the color of the text, as well as the background color of the slide.

- Change the position of the text on the slide. Under the **Template** options, you'll find 11 choices for where the text is placed and whether or not it is animated. Some of the animations include styles like scrolling credits, music video, and caption.

- Changing the movie's title is basically updating the text box. You can type text that creates titles, credits, captions, and more. Once you've updated the text field, you're able to see all of your changes in the preview window. This really helps you to have a sense of how your updates look as part of the project.

Figure 9.13   Adding Text to an Image

Used with permission of Google Inc., and Jared Covili.

- You can add text to existing images in an **overlay** style (see Figure 9.13). This means the text will display over the photo below. As you add text, be sure to use a template that allows you to place the text in a good spot to still focus on the images. A nice template for text on top of an image is the Caption—Typewriter. This template adds a solid-colored background to the title to help people see the text.

 A final tip on the Slide tab: If you would like to add more blank title slides, look for the **New Slide** button down near the timeline. By clicking on this button, you'll be able to add slides with a solid background. This can help if you need to add a longer quote or want to emphasize a particular point in your project.

The Clips Tab

The third and final editing control for movies is the **Clips** tab. This tab has one major function—allowing you to select additional clips for your project.

1. To search for more content, click on the **Get More** button located along the top left side of the tab.

2. Just as when you started the movie, if you're looking for additional photos and video clips, you'll need to add them to the Selection Tray.

Once the clips are in the tray, you'll see an option to return **Back to Movie Maker.**

3. Now that you've gathered the new photos and videos, you'll find that all the clips are placed in the Clips panel.

4. To add them to the actual movie, you'll need to select a clip or clips and click on the **Add** button. This will take your clips down to the timeline where they will become part of the project.

Saving and Sharing Your Movie

Once you've edited your project, it's time to complete the movie by rendering it into a final video. You can save your video regardless of which editing tab you're on.

Figure 9.14 Sharing Options for Movies

Saving

1. At the bottom of each screen, you'll find three options for completing your project: Close the project, Share to YouTube, or Create Movie.

2. When you click on **Close,** Picasa will prompt you to save what you've done as a draft. This gives you the chance to return to your project later. Once a project is saved as a draft, you'll find it back in Picasa's library inside of the Projects folder.

3. To return to the edit mode, click on the draft, and you'll have a choice to **Edit Movie.**

Sharing

1. Selecting **YouTube** will open an upload window.

2. You'll use your Google account to log in to YouTube. Since YouTube is part of the Google tool library, your Gmail address and password will work as a login.

3. After providing a title for the movie and creating a keyword tag, you'll be able to upload your video. It takes a few minutes for the upload to finish, but you've now successfully shared your video online through YouTube.

4. YouTube provides a public or private option for saving your new video (see Figure 9.14). Choosing **public** means your video is searchable in the YouTube library. When you pick **private** as your upload setting, you'll be in control of who is able to view the video,

The **Create Movie** button renders a finished version of your project. The new video is saved to your computer in the Picasa folder—by default, this should be found in the Pictures folder. Videos created in Picasa are MOV files (with a .mov extension) and are played using the Quick Time Player.

■ PICASA WEB ALBUM

A few years ago, Picasa developed a service to help you back up and share your photos online. The Picasa Web Album provides users with free storage for their photos and videos. Now, I know this can be a bit confusing the first time you hear about it, but it's important to keep the two sides of Picasa in the right framework.

- Picasa is the downloadable program for organizing and editing your photos.
- Picasa Web Album is an online storage area where you can upload and share your photos.

Picasa Web Album and Google+

Recently, as noted in Chapter 7, Google+ has been added to the Google library of tools. One of its features is the ability to share photos with your contacts. The photos you upload in Picasa Web Album will now be accessible through Google+. This means your photos can be accessible in both locations.

To access your photos in Google+,

1. Go to Google.com.

2. Log in with your Google account.

3. Click on the **More** link.

4. Select **Photos** from the drop-down menu.

To access your photos in Picasa Web Album,

1. Go to www.picasaweb.com.

2. Log in with your Google account.

It's important to note that your privacy settings will carry over from Picasa Web Album to Google+. Also, any tags or albums you create in one program will be available in the other. Let's learn more about the Picasa Web Album.

Why Use the Picasa Web Album?

If the idea of posting photos online seems a bit overwhelming, let's look at the advantages.

Backup

We've gotten so reliant on our desktops or laptops that a good deal of our lives is stored on their hard drives. Imagine having your computer's hard drive crash with years of digital photos stored within. This is a problem waiting to happen for thousands of us. So, what do we do? Sure, we can burn photos to a disc, or copy them onto our external hard drives, but those solutions are all on-site, meaning they're stored in the same location as our computer. Most people don't have a good system for backing up their photos off-site.

Picasa Web Album gives you a secure site where you can store your pictures and protect them in an off-site environment. It provides a great deal of "peace of mind" knowing that you'll be able to enjoy your images, even in case of a computer emergency.

Storage

Picasa Web Album provides you with 1 GB of free storage for your photos. Depending on the size of your images, you can upload a few hundred photos to store online. As mentioned previously, if you find yourself needing additional storage, Google provides 20 GB for $5 a year.

With 1 GB of storage, you should have plenty of room to place your school- and curriculum-related photos, as well as many of your personal photos. Don't forget, you can share digital video, too, in addition to your digital images.

Sharing

One of the fun aspects of having your photos online is the ability to share your images with others. This is one of the misunderstood aspects of storing materials online—everything you store in Picasa Web Album is not actually available for the world to see. *You* decide which photos you want to share publicly and which images you want to remain private.

As you upload your photos to Picasa Web Album, you can select your level of privacy (see Figure 9.15). Your choices include the following:

Figure 9.15 Picasa Web Album's Privacy Settings

- **Public on the Web**—These photos are included in Google's searching database. Images may be found by searching for their titles, keywords, or by your name.
- **Anyone with the Link**—Like the name implies, if you provide someone with the link to a photo, he or she will have access to the photo or group of photos.
- **Private**—These photos are only available to the owner. The images are intended to be online for backup purpose only.

Sharing allows you to provide access for parents to classroom photos that have likely not been seen in students' homes. One of the advantages of sharing the photos online is the chance to let parents see some of the great things their kids are doing at school. Whether it's the term project, group presentation, class fieldtrip, club activity, school athletic team, or even just everyday photos around the halls of the school, sharing photos in a controlled setting builds a sense of community that's amazing to witness.

Picasa Web Album Basics

Organizing Photos

One of the best things about the Picasa Web Album is that it can mirror the same structure you've already created in Picasa. In addition, any faces, locations, or tags you've applied to your images in Picasa will be transferred to the Picasa Web Album. This will save you a ton of time and duplicated effort.

Uploading and Syncing Images

1. You can upload new photos directly into the web album. Once logged into your account, you'll find a button to **Upload** photos.

2. You'll then be prompted to add the images to an existing album or to create a new album for the pictures. Once you've decided where the photos will be stored, the system works about like attaching a file to an e-mail.

3. Browse to find your desired photo, and select the image for upload. You can actually upload five images at a time using the direct upload to the Picasa Web Album. Once you've selected the image(s) for upload, click **OK** for the transfer to take place.

The other common way to add photos to the Picasa Web Album is to "sync" the images directly from Picasa. The process couldn't be simpler.

1. Once you've arranged your photos into a folder or album in Picasa, choose the **Sync to Web** option found in the upper right corner of the group of images. In a matter of minutes, your photos will be synced with your Picasa Web Album. *Note: In the latest update of Picasa for the PC, the sync to Web option sends images directly to Google +, not to the Picasa Web Album.*

2. Pay attention to the default settings for the transfer. You may want to adjust the size and visibility options for your images. If this is the case, click on the **Change Settings** button when the sync manager appears.

Once an album or folder has been set to **Sync to Web,** any editing done to the picture will automatically sync to the online version of the photo. This applies to tags, basic edits, or any other type of correction. It works great and ensures you'll have the edited version of your photos in both locations.

Figure 9.16   Download from Web to Computer

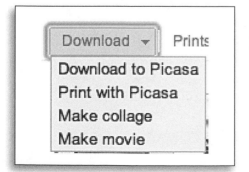

Downloading Your Web Albums Back to Your Computer

Picasa Web is a great way to back up your photos, but how do you actually get the images from the web to your computer? It only takes a few simple steps to go from computer disaster to enjoying your pictures again (see Figure 9.16).

1. Select the album you wish to download to the desktop version of Picasa.

2. Click on the **Download** link.

3. Choose **Download to Picasa.**

This not only serves as a form of backup, but teachers and students can use this system as a way to transfer from one computer to another. Just upload the images at home, and you can access or edit them at school.

Sharing Photos in the Picasa Web Album

Earlier, we discussed how sharing an album provides parents and students with access to photos you've taken at school. Let's not forget that students can share their digital photo project with you as well. Students sharing their photos with an instructor can provide a secure way to evaluate their work and manage classroom projects.

To share images with others,

1. Select the album you'd like to share (or have your students select one of their albums to share).

2. Click on the **Share** button.

3. Enter the e-mail address of the person or persons with whom you'd like to share the album. You can enter e-mail addresses directly or choose from your Gmail contacts.

4. Once someone accepts an invitation to an album of photos, he or she will find the images in his or her own Picasa Web Album under the Recent Activity heading. If more images are added to the album, you'll instantly see them in your Picasa Web.

5. Not only can you share your images with parents and students, but you can also actually allow others to add to your collection of photos. To create a collaborative gallery when sharing your images, be sure to check the **Let People I Share with Collaborate** box.

This is a fun way to create a community drop box of photos from a field trip or other classroom activity. If parents or students want to contribute to the album, now they can!

Community Photos in Picasa Web Album

With thousands of people uploading their photos to the Web using the Picasa Web Album, there are millions of images being stored in the Google database. Many people choose to keep their photos private, so others cannot see their images. Still, there are thousands of images that are available to the public. (see Figure 9.17.)

Teachers are always looking for images they can use with their students as part of multimedia projects in class. When you first arrive in the Picasa Web Album, you'll find photos by doing the following:

1. Click on the **Explore** tab along the top left of the screen.

2. Use the **Search** box at the top right of the screen.

3. Type your topic, and you'll find hundreds of images that come back from your search.

4. Remember to be specific with your search parameters. The use of quotes around your search term will help narrow the results.

However, just because you have images in the search results doesn't mean you can use them any way you want.

Figure 9.17   Finding Public Images in Picasa Web Album

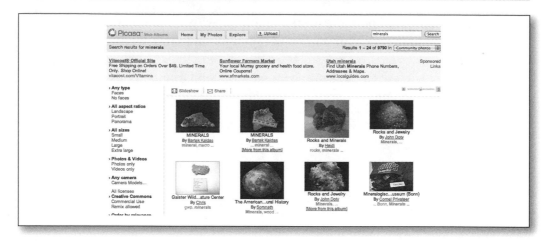

Photos in the public database can still carry a few different copyright protections for their owners. When you first load your images, there is an option to add the **Creative Commons** license to the photo. Some of the different protections this includes are the following: Viewing rights only, Use only with permission and citation, or General public use. You can decide what level of access you'd like to give the public. Also, you and your students need to respect the rights of others by following the permissions others have established for their photos. It's a good chance to teach your students about copyright and fair use policies.

Project Idea: Creating and Sharing Slideshows

NETS-S Standard 2 Objective c

Students use digital media and environments to communicate and work collaboratively, including at a distance, to support individual learning and contribute to the learning of others. Students communicate information and ideas effectively to multiple audiences using a variety of media and formats. (ISTE, 2007)

Slideshows in the Picasa Web Album can be a fun way to share images, but you can also use the slideshow as an instructional tool. If you want to display the images as a form of visual quiz, you can ask questions about the photos and assess the students' understanding of the object or event.

In addition to showing photos as an assessment tool, a slideshow you embed on your website or blog can help you engage students and parents in classroom activities. You can control which images you use and how the slideshow appears on your classroom website.

Displaying a Slideshow

To display a slideshow, do the following in Picasa Web Album:

1. Click on the album of photos you'd like to show your students.
2. Select the **Slideshow** button along the top left of your menu choices.

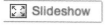

3. The slideshow will play automatically, but you can adjust the time each image displays.

4. You can also choose to advance the slide manually. This is a good tool to pause for questions and classroom discussion.

Creating a Slideshow for Your Website or Blog

1. Select the album of photos you plan to use for your slideshow. You can only use Public albums for an embeddable slideshow. If your album's images are private, adjust the **Visibility** settings under the **Edit** menu with **Album Properties**.

2. Click on the **Link to this Album** option located along the right side of the screen.

3. Select the **Embed Slideshow** option.

4. A display window will appear that provides you with several options for your slideshow including size, captions, and an auto run feature.

5. Copy the code for the slideshow, and paste it into your blog or website.

Picasa is an amazing tool that is sure to bring out the creativity in your students. When used as part of a Google classroom, Picasa can build community among parents, students, and the schools. You can engage visual learners in innovative ways. Students see so many incredible things in the world around them, and you can help them visualize their learning, both inside and outside of the classroom.

MORE IDEAS FOR GOING GOOGLE

Other Photo Project Ideas

- Create a Movie Trailer for a Book—Using the Movie feature in Picasa, have your students create a multimedia photo trailer of a book instead of a traditional book report.

  o Scan images from the actual text, or find images online.
  o Import the images into Picasa.
  o Edit the images and add captions to the photos using the **Text** tool.
  o Arrange the photos for the trailer in the **Selection Tray.**
  o Select the **Movie** option from the tools along the bottom of the screen.
  o Create a dramatic movie feel for your project by adding an appropriate song in the **Movie** tab. Select the **Load** button to browse through the music.
  o Create title slides and credits using the **Slide** tab. Remember, you can add text to blank slides or overlay text onto your images. Choose important quotes from the book. Introduce main characters. Provide an interesting fact about the book.
  o When they're finished, have students upload their projects to YouTube or use the **Create Movie** button to complete the project.

(Continued)

(Continued)

- Create a Classroom Seating Chart—This is a good management strategy for your classroom. A visual seating chart can help you learn students' names faster by having the picture associated with the student.

  ○ Import the students' images into Picasa.
  ○ Add names to each student photo by using the **Text** tool, under the **Basic Fixes** editing tab.
  ○ Add the students' photos to the **Selection Tray.** Arrange the photos in place according to their chosen seats.
  ○ Select the **Collage** tool.
  ○ Choose the **Contact Sheet** as your collage option.
  ○ The images will arrange in a grid that should mirror the alignment of the desks in your classroom.

TIPS FOR THE GOOGLE CLASSROOM

- Be sure to get parental permission when taking pictures of students, especially when planning to use the images online. Your district will have a policy regarding using digital photos of students. Make sure you understand the policy and follow it.
- Take advantage of the cameras the students already have. Research says that over 75% of students from 12–19 have a cell phone in the pocket every school day. With budgetary restrictions and limited resources, it's important to note that those cell phones are digital cameras the students can use for class projects!
- A fun way to get the students involved is to have a classroom photographer. Make this a rotating position that gets to use the class camera to document what happened during the period or activity. Kids will see things that adults never imagined (and that's a good thing).

10

YouTube

YouTube has truly revolutionized the Internet over the past decade. We now have access to images and stories that we never imagined possible. Students are "firsthand" witnesses to world events, and they have the ability to contribute their thoughts and feelings about what they are seeing to the global community. YouTube has given unprecedented access to the globe and has influenced billions of people. And yet, it is banned in many schools and even colleges across the United States, as well as in a number of countries. Why?

It would seem that access to this site is one of the most polarizing topics in school today. No matter where you stand on the issue of open access to YouTube for students, one thing is undeniable—YouTube isn't going away, and its impact will only get stronger. Many educators have embraced the site as another resource that can be used to enhance instruction and help students learn. Video is a tremendous teaching tool, and students are excited by visual instruction.

> Students today do tend to have shorter attention spans than ever before because their minds are bombarded with extraordinary amounts of visual stimulus from a young age. By using their fascination with this medium, and showing relevant course material that both directly and indirectly relates, we as educators can help bridge the academic rift that often stretches between students and their texts. (Graves, Juel, & Graves, 2006)

In this chapter, we'll explore the basics of how teachers can use YouTube to share their own original content for students by uploading their videos to YouTube. You'll learn how creating a YouTube channel can help you organize your content and provide links to other YouTube content. The chapter will show you how to help student create a "mashup" video where they remix existing content into a brand new movie.

TYPES OF VIDEOS ON YOUTUBE ■

Current Events: The media maximizes YouTube as an outlet for sharing current news stories. You'll find the latest international news stories as told by Reuters, the AP, the BBC, *New York Times,* and more. National news outlets using YouTube include CNN, ABC, NBC, CBS, PBS, Fox News, and so on. It isn't just the media outlets, either—national and local governments also share their messages using YouTube. Go check the White House Channel, and you'll be able to view behind-the-scenes content from President Obama and the White House staff.

However, news isn't just being reported by the professional sources; everyday people like you and me are recording firsthand accounts of history and sharing it through YouTube. Often, eyewitness accounts are shared across the globe as individuals upload their cell phone videos on YouTube.

Inspirational: Teachers understand the role that video can play in helping inspire students. On YouTube, you'll find all kinds of inspirational clips—everything from true-life stories of people overcoming challenges to historical speeches that stirred the nations.

How-to Videos: This is one of the best things about YouTube. With so many students (and teachers) considering themselves visual learners, YouTube is an amazing repository of 3- to 5-minute tutorials about a limitless number of topics. When it comes to technology and software instruction, you can find videos on all of the tools you have access to in your classroom. Want to learn how to use PowerPoint? What about building a classroom website using Dreamweaver? There are hundreds of training videos being created by users for users.

Google Tools Videos: Google has several different channels on YouTube that can help you learn directly about their tools. You'll find information on using Google Docs, Google Earth, Picasa, Blogger, Google Search, iGoogle, Gmail, Google Calendar, and more. These videos are professionally created, and they provide skill development from the very basic to the most advanced.

Student Showcase: Because YouTube is part of one's Google account, users are invited to share their videos with the public. This makes it a great venue for students to share their school projects with peers, teachers, and parents.

■ ADDING VIDEOS TO YOUTUBE

Finding useful videos on YouTube is terrific, but you'll uncover the real influence of YouTube when you and your students share your own content with peers, parents, colleagues, and—potentially—the world. You and your students will need Google accounts in order to upload your videos to YouTube. The process is then fairly simple:

1. Go to YouTube.com. Sign in with your Google account.

2. Click on **Upload.**

   Upload video   or   **Record from webcam**

3. There are two major ways to add video to YouTube. One is by uploading a completed video using the **Upload Video** button. The other option is to record a video using a webcam. YouTube has buttons that will guide you through each of these choices.

When Uploading Video you there are a few guidelines to consider:

- Videos being uploaded to YouTube can be no longer than 15 minutes and no larger than 2 GB in size.
- Videos can come from a variety of formats, but the most common file types include MPG, AVI, M4V, MOV, and WMV.
- Videos must not contain any commercial content that one does not have permission to share. This includes movies, TV shows, music, and live concerts.

To upload a video, you can

1. Drag and drop the clip into the upload window.

2. Or you can browse to your desired video using the **Upload video** button.

Once you find the video and select it, an upload screen will appear. The video should already be uploading to YouTube, but you'll need to provide some basic information about the content. Some of the elements you'll add to your videos include name, description, tags, category, and privacy setting. You can control all of these settings, particularly the privacy setting. Your three choices for privacy include

- Public—where the video is available to all YouTube users
- Unlisted—the video is only available to those with the URL
- Private—the video's owner provides access to the video by adding selected viewers.

Recording Video

If you connect a webcam to your computer, YouTube makes creating your own video simple:

1. Click on the **Record from Webcam** link when you're on the YouTube upload page.

2. YouTube will launch a page that should automatically look for your webcam and connect it to the YouTube uploader. You'll need to make sure your webcam is working and connected to the computer.

3. Click the **Ready to Record** button. You'll find your video instantly starts recording. A webcam video is a great way to provide a response to someone else's video or to share your own ideas about a particular topic.

4. Once you're done recording your video, click on the red **Stop** button in the lower left corner of the controls.

5. YouTube will provide you with three options: **Publish** to your channel, **Preview** the video, or **Re-Record** the video (see Figure 10.1).

Figure 10.1   Video Options in YouTube

Used with permission of Google Inc., and Jared Covili.

■ YOUR YOUTUBE CHANNEL

Once you start adding videos to YouTube, they become part of your YouTube channel. This is a repository of all your uploaded content. This is a great way to back up your videos, and it also becomes a convenient way to share that content with parents, students, and colleagues. Perhaps the easiest way to share related content is with a playlist from your YouTube channel (see below).

Here are a few things to remember about your YouTube channel:

- Your channel can be public or private (see Figure 10.2). The default setting is public, but if you want to keep the channel unavailable, choose "no" on the **Make Channel Visible** option in the Settings tab.

Figure 10.2   YouTube Channel Settings

- As a teacher, a fun option for your channel is to declare yourself a "guru," thus letting people know of your educational background. If you aren't interested in that label, the basic status is "user."

- You can choose what content to display on your channel. Playlists, subscriptions, favorites, and comments are all possible content for your YouTube channel (see Figure 10.3).

Figure 10.3 Types of YouTube Content for Your Channel

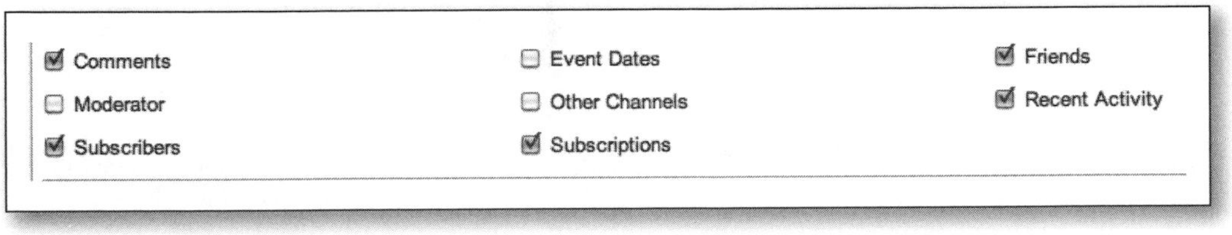

☑ Comments   ☐ Event Dates   ☑ Friends
☐ Moderator   ☐ Other Channels   ☑ Recent Activity
☑ Subscribers   ☑ Subscriptions

Creating a Playlist

Once you have your YouTube channel filled with content, a nice way to manage your videos is by organizing clips on a topic or concept into a specific "playlist." With the average video in YouTube being 3–5 minutes long, playlists are extremely valuable to help keep a series of video tutorials together in one location. Another advantage to playlists is that they can be shared or embedded on a website. To create a playlist from your YouTube channel,

1. Choose the desired video from your Uploads or your Favorite videos from your YouTube channel.

2. Select the **Playlists** button from below the Preview screen on your YouTube channel.

3. Create a new playlist by typing a **Playlist Name** in the provided space.

4. Click **Create Playlist.**

5. You can add a video to an existing playlist by choosing the appropriate playlist and clicking **Add to Playlist.**

Downloading a YouTube Video

I know, I know. How can I write a section about downloading a YouTube video with so much debate about access to YouTube while at school? There are some ways to avoid the debate, and to use the great materials found on the site. Let's look at a few different downloading tools that can help you show educational videos to your students.

Real Player Downloader

This is a free application that allows you to download YouTube videos to your computer (see Figure 10.4). Once the program is installed on your computer, it will automatically open when an available YouTube video is in your browser.

To download a copy of the video, click the **Download** button.

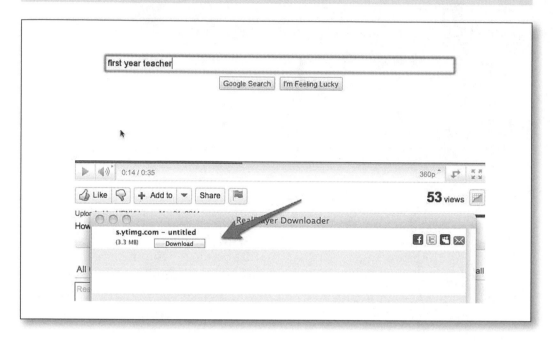

Figure 10.4 Using Real Player Downloader

File Wiggler

Filewiggler.com is a free website that allows you to download a YouTube video to your computer. You'll need to copy the URL for the video in YouTube and then go to filewiggler.com. It takes just four steps to set up your conversion.

1. Paste the URL for your YouTube video in the space provided.

2. Choose the format you plan to use for the conversion. There are several options to choose from, and they include both desktop and mobile platforms.

3. Provide an e-mail address to File Wiggler so they can notify you when the conversion in complete.

4. Agree to the terms, and submit the conversion.

A few minutes after you submit your YouTube version for download, you'll receive an e-mail address that contains a link for your video. Follow the link, and download your video.

YouTube Downloader Extension in Firefox

Another great downloading tool is found in the browser Firefox. To install this extension, you'll need to be using the Firefox browser. (It's a free download if you don't already have it on your computer.)

1. Open Firefox and click on the **Tools** link along the top of your screen.

2. Select the **Add-ons** option from the drop-down menu.

3. Under the **Get Add-ons** tab, search for **YouTube Downloader.** There are several different downloading tools available. The one I prefer is the Flash Video Downloader (YouTube Downloader)—you'll recognize it by the blue download arrow.

4. Once you install the downloader, it will appear in your toolbar in Firefox. The arrow will be "grayed out" until you arrive on a video in YouTube. The arrow will turn blue once a video becomes available.

Figure 10.5 Firefox's YouTube Downloader Extension

5. The downloader will provide you with different options for saving the file. The primary option for playback on your computer is the MP4 file type.

6. Click the **Download** button, and a few seconds later you'll have a downloaded copy of the YouTube video.

Project Idea: Creating a "Mashup" Video in YouTube

Much of the content on YouTube is only viewable, but students want to use video to *create* new content. One of the lesser-known tools in YouTube is the **Video Editor.** The Video Editor is a free tool in your YouTube account that allows you to edit various clips and produce an entirely new "mashup." The Video Editor allows you to

- Combine multiple videos, thus creating a mashup of your clips.
- Edit the video by trimming the beginning or end of your clips
- Add a music soundtrack from YouTube's AutoSwap collection of songs
- Create new videos that can be published to your YouTube account.

> **NETS-S Standard 1 Objective a**
>
> Students demonstrate creative thinking, construct knowledge, and develop innovative products and processes using technology. Students apply existing knowledge to generate new ideas, products, or processes. (ISTE, 2007)

Getting Started With the YouTube Editor

The easiest way to access the YouTube editor is by going directly to www.youtube.com/editor. You can also access the editor through your account settings, but we won't worry about that right now. To create a mashup video, you'll need to have the clips already uploaded to your YouTube account.

Figure 10.6 Add Video to Storyboard

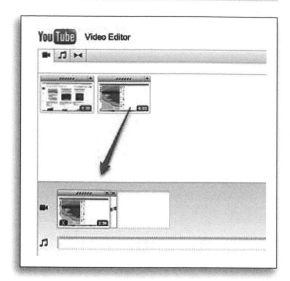

Adding Video to Your New Mashup

1. In the **Media Picker**, select the clip(s) you'd like to edit.

2. Click the **plus icon** (+) on the side of the clip. This will add the clip to the storyboard. You can also drag and drop the clip down to the storyboard. (see Figure 10.6.)

3. You can add from 1–7 clips to your new video.

Editing Your Clips

There are three basics edits you can perform in the YouTube Video Editor: trimming, rotating, and brightness/stabilization (see Figure 10.7). One of the basic edits dealing with digital video is trimming. This allows you to pick the start and end points of any of the clips you plan to use in your mashup.

To trim a clip in Editor,

Figure 10.7 Editing Controls

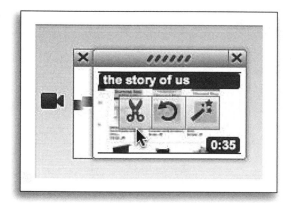

1. Hover over the clip and click the **Scissors** or **trim** icon.

2. An editing window will appear.

3. To shorten the clip, select the **Clip Trimmer** at the beginning and/or end of the video's frames (see Figure 10.8).

4. Drag the gray trimmer to your desired start or end point of the clip that you'd like to trim.

5. Once you've cut your clip, click the **Save** button. This will store your changed clip and send you back to the main editing screen.

You can edit all the clips that are currently in the Clip Trimmer. Remember, each clip is edited individually, and you'll need to click the Save button when you've finished trimming a particular clip.

Clip Trimmer Basics

Figure 10.8 Using the Clip Trimmer

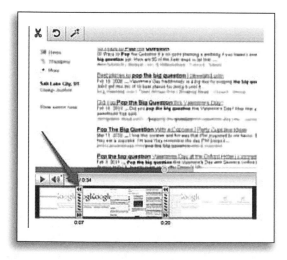

- The inside of the gray bar is the point of the actual edit. Don't worry about the outer edge of the Clip Trimmer; it's the inner edge that determines your edit points.
- You can trim a clip to a 15th of a second. For longer videos, if you click the **Nudge** buttons, this will nudge the trimmer forward or backward a 15th of a second from its current position.

- When you add a video clip to the storyboard, the video that appears in the player is the *actual* video from YouTube.com. This video loads and plays like any YouTube video.

Beyond trimming your clips, the YouTube Editor also allows you to *rotate* your clips. Click on **the curled arrow** icon, and you'll be prompted to rotate the video clockwise or counter clockwise.

If your clips are shaky and difficult to watch, the YouTube Editor has a *stabilize* option. Click on the **magic wand** icon, and you'll find a check box for stabilization. You can adjust the level of your stabilization by using the slider provided.

Adding an Audio Soundtrack

You can add a new audio track to your video in the Video Editor. Here's how:

1. In the Media Picker, click the **Audio Tab**. You'll then see audio options appear. These audio tracks come from YouTube's AudioSwap library.

2. Browse the AudioSwap tracks by genre and artist, or by typing a query into the AudioSwap search bar.

Figure 10.9 Music Appears in the Storyboard

3. To preview the listed audio tracks, hover your mouse over the audio track in question and click the **Play** button. A preview will then play for you.

4. You can add an audio track to your clip in one of two ways: One way is to click the **plus** icon (+) on the audio track. Alternatively, you can drag and drop the audio track into the audio section of the storyboard.

5. The audio track cannot be trimmed in the YouTube Video Editor. This means you cannot select portions of the soundtrack; the audio will start at its beginning and will end when the video ends.

6. Deleting an audio track is simple. Just click the **X** icon on the audio track in the storyboard. You can also replace the audio track by dragging another track from the clips down to the storyboard. The new track will immediately replace the old track.

7. The video has its own audio as well as a soundtrack. You can adjust the volume to only play the soundtrack, to play just the video's audio, or move the slider somewhere in between for a mixture of both inputs.

Creating Transitions

Since we're combining two or more videos into our "mashup," adding transitions is an effective way to blend the videos together (see Figure 10.10).

Figure 10.10 Transition Option

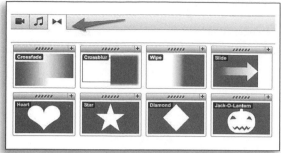

1. Click on the **Transition** icon along the top set of tools. It resembles a bow tie.

2. Choose your desired transition from the list that appears.

3. Drag the transition in between the two clips in the storyboard.

Publishing Your Final Video

The final steps in creating your "mashup" video involve naming the new project and publishing the video to your YouTube channel (see Figure 10.11). The controls for this are found in the top right corner of the editor.

1. Type the name for your "mashup" video in the widow provided.

2. Click the **Publish** button.

Figure 10.11 Publishing Your New Video

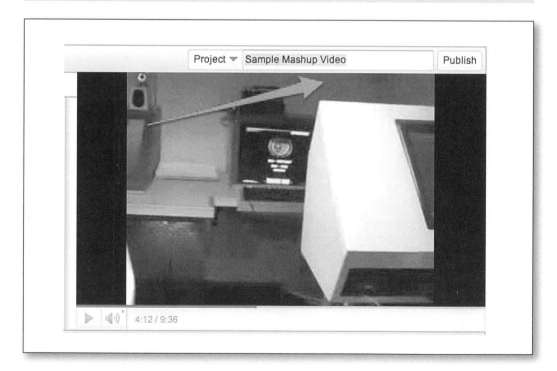

Depending on the new video's length, it may take a few minutes to process. You can check on the video's processing status on the My Videos page of your account. Once completed, the new video you created will have an entirely separate URL of its own.

Project Idea: Creating a Search Story

Search Stories combines two of Google's best-known products, Google Search and YouTube. Imagine having your students tell stories using search results and music.

1. Go to www.YouTube.com/SearchStories. You'll find a gallery of SearchStories from different YouTube users.

2. Click on the **Create your own** icon.

3. The Search Stories editor will load. You'll start in the **Write** mode of the editor.

4. To write your story, you can choose up to seven different search terms. To help you create your story, Google provides the following tips:

   a. Try using the different kinds of search (maps, images, products) to add variety to your story.

   b. Use different search features to help get a big plot point across quickly and clearly.

   c. Try and build a narrative arc that ends with the last search delivering a surprise or, better yet, the beginning of a new story.

   d. Make it personal! Tell the story of something you accomplished, fell in love with, or discovered. Or make it about aliens. That's cool, too. (www.youtube.com/searchstories)

5. Depending on your type of search, several different results will display. A Web search will display basic website search results. Images will utilize Google's image search. Different types of search include Web, Images, Maps, News, Blog, Product, and Books. Each of these will give your story a different look and feel.

6. You can preview your search results from each search term in the window at the bottom of the screen.

7. Once you are satisfied with your terms, click on the **Next** button to add music to your story.

8. In the Music tab, you'll find a wide variety of emotional music genres. Pick from Romantic to Sci-Fi, and everything in between. For each genre of music, you'll have three different songs to pick from. You can preview the songs before making your final choice.

9. The editor will compile a preview of your finished video. At this point, you can go back and edit the search results or music.

> Edit Story   Change Music

10. Once you're content with the project, your final option is to publish the video to your YouTube channel. Before you publish your video,

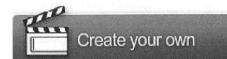

> **NETS S Standard I**
> **Objective a**
>
> Students demonstrate creative thinking, construct knowledge, and develop innovative products and processes using technology. Students apply existing knowledge to generate new ideas, products, or processes. (ISTE, 2007)

be sure to add a **Title** of your story. You can also add a **Description** of your story to provide a brief summary of the project.

11. Click **Upload to YouTube**, and you're done (see Figure 10.12). Your video will appear on your YouTube channel within a few moments.

Figure 10.12 Uploading Your Search Story to YouTube

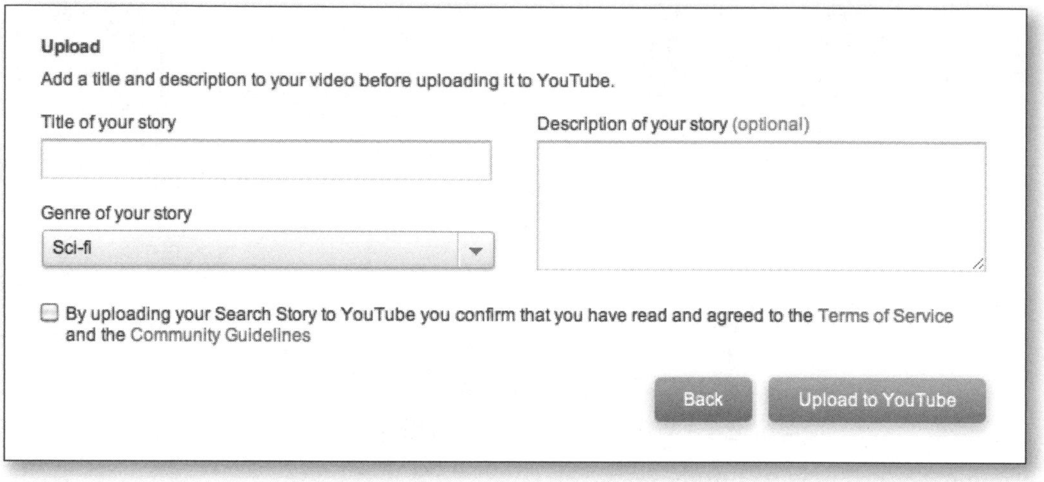

MORE IDEAS FOR GOING GOOGLE

Other video projects can include:

- YouTube has a repository of videos just for students and teachers. Go to www.youtube.com/education and you'll find a collection of videos in the Primary and Secondary Education category. Here you can find video tutorials from sources like the Khan Academy. You can also find resources from PBS and TedTalks.
- A new YouTube resource for your school is found at www.youtube.com/schools. At this site, your school can create a free account where administrators can choose from a selection of educational videos that can be shared with students. The videos are aligned with national standards and allow teachers to create playlists of videos they can use in instruction.
- Subscribe to other educators' YouTube channels. Part of the allure of YouTube is the social side of sharing videos. By finding and subscribing to other teachers' YouTube channels, you'll be developing a PLN (Personal Learning Network) with educators from around the globe. These relationships can be very beneficial, as your PLN can help you find additional resources.
- Check out DemoSlam.com for an entertaining look at users' video tutorials on a variety of Google products. These videos provide lots of creative ways to use tools like Google Search, Google Earth, Google Maps, and more. For a fun classroom activity, have your students brainstorm possible DemoSlam videos they can create.

TIPS FOR THE GOOGLE CLASSROOM

- Preview videos before using them to determine appropriate and relevant content. Many YouTube videos get right to the point, but others may need to be scanned to ensure you only show the relevant content to strengthen your curriculum. Even though students like watching videos, no one wants to watch a long clip that doesn't relate to what he or she is learning.
- Downloading a video before showing it in class provides you a security net with your local network. Rather than relying on the Internet to be "up and running" at the very moment you need it, downloading the videos in advance provides you with the assurance that you'll have access to your clip.
- Be sensitive to the guidelines and policies of your local school or district. Just because there are many good things about YouTube for education, there are also many justified concerns that local officials have about opening up a public video service to young people. Be an advocate for effective instruction using video, but don't be overbearing with demands for access.

Part III

Critical Thinking and Problem Solving

Modern learners have access to so much more information than previous generations. One of the biggest challenges to students today isn't finding information; it's evaluating the information they've found. This is reflected in the following guidelines for 21st century learning skills.

Students should be able to

- Effectively analyze and evaluate evidence, arguments, claims, and beliefs.
- Analyze and evaluate major alternative points of view.
- Synthesize and make connections between information and arguments.
- Interpret information and draw conclusions based on the best analysis.
- Reflect critically on learning experiences and processes (Partnership for 21st Century Skills, 2004, n.p.).

As we work with students it is more important now, than ever before, that we help students uncover information rather than simply trying to cover your material. This is reflected in the following quote from *Teaching the 21st Century Learner.*

With the rate of information growth continuously accelerating, higher education today must place less emphasis on the amount of material memorized and more weight on making connections, thinking through issues, and solving problems. We must discard the notions that schools can teach everything every student will need to know to be successful in their field of choice. We must move beyond the old university model where the primary challenge of learning was to absorb a vast array of specific information. (Rogers, Runyon, Starrett, & Von Holzen, 2006, n.p.)

IS GOOGLE MAKING US STUPID? ∎

Google's primary focus since its inception has been that of searching. Google is a place to find information. While Google's search engine has helped students find a great deal of content on the Internet, one of the largest issues surrounding the use of Google in education is the notion that the search engine is "making us stupid" (Carr, 2008). Many in education feel that Google searches have halted our students' ability to think critically and to solve problems. Take this example of author Nicholas Carr, reflecting upon his ability to process new information in the Google era.

> Over the past few years I've had an uncomfortable sense that someone, or something, has been tinkering with my brain, remapping the neural circuitry, reprogramming the memory. My mind isn't going—so far as I can tell—but it's changing. I'm not thinking the way I used to think. I can feel it most strongly when I'm reading. Immersing myself in a book or a lengthy article used to be easy. My mind would get caught up in the narrative or the turns of the argument, and I'd spend hours strolling through long stretches of prose. That's rarely the case anymore. Now my concentration often starts to drift after two or three pages. I get fidgety, lose the thread, begin looking for something else to do. I feel as if I'm always dragging my wayward brain back to the text. The deep reading that used to come naturally has become a struggle. (n.p.)

Is this the case? Is Google at the root of our students' inability to focus on in-depth information and to solve problems using the data found in a typical search?

In a 2008 research study, Dr. Gary Small (quoted in Dretzin, 2010) of UCLA explored the amount of brain activity someone has while conducting a Google search (see Figure 11.1). The findings were staggering. There was almost twice as much brain activity from researching on Google versus reading a book. Small noted that there is a great deal of activity taking place in the frontal lobe of the brain. "This is the decision-making part of the brain. It makes sense because we know we're making lots of decisions when we're searching online" (n.p.).

Figure 11.1   Difference in Brain Activity While Reading a Book vs. Searching With Google

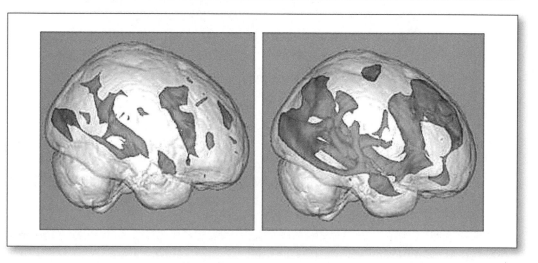

Source: http://www.newsroom.ucla.edu/portal/ucla/srp-view.aspx?id=34812

So, maybe Google isn't really making our students stupid. Rather, it looks like students make hundreds of decisions during the time when they are conducting searches. Students are using the search results to determine relevance to their topic; they are establishing relationships between various sites' content. Google is helping our students reach additional skills for 21st century learners such as the following:

- Use various types of reasoning (inductive, deductive, etc.) as appropriate to the situation.
- Analyze how parts of a whole interact with each other to produce overall outcomes in complex systems (Partnership for 21st Century Skills, 2004, n.p.).

In this section, we'll explore how Google can play a role in developing critical thinking skills and help students solve problems. We'll look at how Google can be used to access information and utilize it to improve their researching for school. As part of our discussion, we'll focus on Google's search engine and aggregating information with Google.

11

Google as a Searching Tool

---- ❧ ----

FIVE THINGS TO KNOW ABOUT GOOGLE SEARCH

1. Using Google's Advanced Search will improve and focus search results.
2. Google can search for specific types of files including images, PowerPoints, PDFs, and more.
3. Google Translate translates between dozens of languages.
4. Google Custom Search can provide teachers with a content search on specific teacher-selected websites.
5. Google's time-saving searches can help your students find quick reference material on the Internet.

---- ❧ ----

It's the number one way in which you use Google. Before there was Gmail, Docs, or Earth, there was Google's search engine. Google—one simple site that changed everything we do on the web on a daily basis.

It is estimated that Google performs over 34,000 searches per second. That's 2 million per minute, 121 million per hour, 3 billion per day, and 88 billion per month (McGee, 2010, n.p.). So the question is, why? What makes the Google search engine the first choice for finding information for millions of people every day? According to Consumersearch.com (2011), Google remains the world's number one search engine for a number of reasons.

> **NETS-S Standard 3 Objective b**
>
> Students apply digital tools to gather, evaluate, and use information. Students locate, organize, analyze, evaluate, synthesize, and ethically use information from a variety of sources and media. (ISTE, 2007)

Google remains the favorite choice of both users and expert reviewers, who praise its speed, relevant results and ease of use. Besides its core web search, Google also has such cutting-edge features as the ability to search images, videos and blogs, and one can use Book Search to preview text from Google's selection of digitized books. (n.p.)

155

We love Google for the same reasons as our students: It's easy to find information quickly, from a variety of sources, and in several different media types. With one search engine, we can find websites, PowerPoints, images, videos, blog posts, maps, and more.

Google Search has empowered us as teachers, but more importantly it has transformed our students into knowledge sources as well. Before the Internet and, specifically, before Google, knowledge was the primary domain of the teacher. Now, our students are capable of finding information quickly and contributing more to the classroom conversation.

We all have the opportunity with today's technology to access a great deal of information, and very quickly. You can be sitting there watching TV and somebody might bring up a comment and you can say, 'Let me check that, let me verify that,' and instantly we Bing it or Google it. (Bulley, 2011)

The next few chapters will explore some of the hidden tools included in Google's Advanced Search and Google Custom Search. Each of the tools can help you and your students find the right information on the Internet.

12

Advanced Search

As people search with Google, a common complaint is the number of unrelated searches that come back with the results. When we search, we want to know how to find the most relevant information and how to filter out a lot of the unwanted material that comes in a normal search. Google wants to help you access the content you're looking for, while minimizing unnecessary results. I mean, come on, who really needs access to over 1 billion search results about the food product Spam (see Figure 12.1)?

Boolean searches are a possible solution, but who wants to remember to use plus signs or how to exclude terms from one's search? Google has built in a great solution for maximizing results—the Advanced Search option.

Figure 12.1 Example of Millions of Search Results Using Google

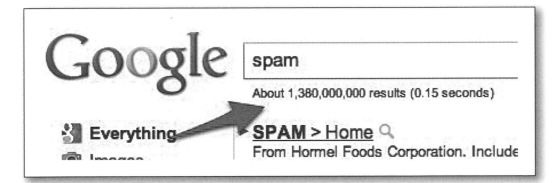

As you start your next search on Google, click on **Advanced Search,** located in the settings (small gear icon) drop-down menu in the top right side of the screen and along side the search bar, depending on your browser. (See Figure 12.2, which follows.)

Figure 12.2 Using the Advanced Search Button

Let's look at how you can reduce search results and find better resources using the Advanced Search feature and a recent national news story. If a student types "Joplin" into the basic Google Search box, the results in Figure 12.3 are what come up.

Like many Google searches, you'll find that mixed in with information about the town of Joplin, Missouri, and the recent tornado there are references to Scott Joplin and Janis Joplin—great topics, but not the information you were looking for with your search.

Figure 12.3 Standard Search Results in Google

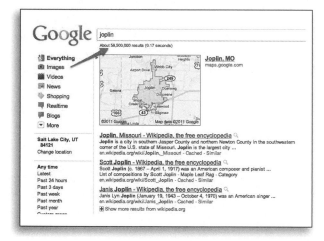

With a basic Google search, any reference that includes the term "Joplin" is part of the results. That's why Janis and Scott Joplin make the list and why you get frustrated with the 58,500,000 other items that returned with the search. We need to get more specific and use better search techniques to help us refine our results.

Now, let's conduct the same search but using the "Keywords" feature of Advanced Search to help us get the results we're looking for (see Figure 12.4).

Figure 12.4 Advanced Search Will Build Your Search With Keywords

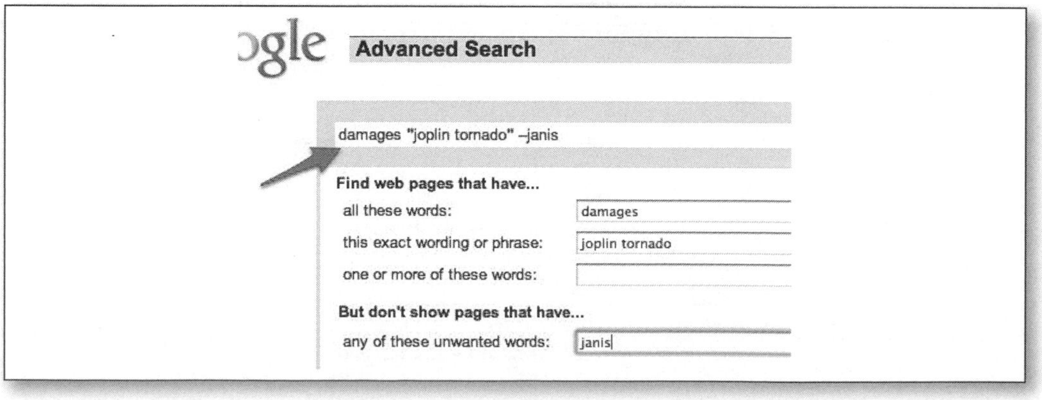

ogle **Advanced Search**

damages "joplin tornado" –janis

Find web pages that have...

all these words: damages

this exact wording or phrase: joplin tornado

one or more of these words:

But don't show pages that have...

any of these unwanted words: janis

ADVANCED SEARCH FEATURES ■

When searching with Google, a few advanced search options will help you and your students get more targeted results. Here are a few tips for getting the most out of your Google searches.

- *Keywords:* In Advanced Search, adding additional terms or keywords is vital to refining your search and making the most relevant sites come to the forefront of your results. You can add keywords in the **all these words** field. This will set the order of your results. Instead of looking for Joplin, Missouri, we're now looking for damages in Joplin (see Figure 12.4).
- *Phrases:* Another important element of searching with Google Advanced Search is linking two words together as a phrase. When you utilize the field **this exact wording or phrase,** your search limits the results to only your keywords when they are listed together. For our example, the results with the phrase "Joplin tornado" are given the top priority in our search. This means anything dealing with the singer Janis Joplin or the composer Scott Joplin won't display in our results.
- *Excluding terms:* Many times, a search will include related terms due to the large amount of material on the web. Another way to refine your search is to exclude pages that have **any of these unwanted words.**

Just using a few simple keyword filters in our search can change the results dramatically. Earlier, we had over 58 million results by using Google Basic Search and the term "Joplin." Now, after using Google's Advanced Search, we have dropped to 1.9 million results. This means we got rid of over 95 percent of unwanted search results (see Figure 12.5). As we go through the list of results, we will find that the top listings all deal directly with damages from the tornado, due to our use of specific keywords.

Figure 12.5   Over 95 Percent of Search Results Are Filtered Out With Advanced Search

damages "joplin tornado" -janis

About 1,950,000 results (0.20 seconds)

FUN SEARCHING TIP—TRY USING THE VOICE SEARCH OPTION IN GOOGLE CHROME

- Click on the **Microphone** icon in the Google Search box.
- Plug in your mic, or use the computer's built-in microphone.
- Say your search term aloud.
- Watch the results come in!

Need More Tools?

As we've just learned, Advanced Search can help you filter your results when you manually type in keywords and phrases. If you continue down the Advanced Search menu options, though, you'll find a heading that says **Need more tools?** Here, you'll have access to filters by site, file type, reading level, and more (see Figure 12.6). Let's explore a few of these in greater detail.

Figure 12.6 More Tools in Advanced Search

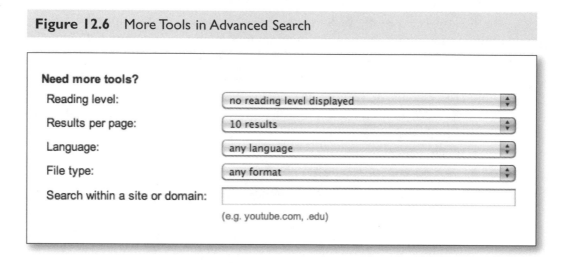

Reading level: no reading level displayed

Results per page: 10 results

Language: any language

File type: any format

Search within a site or domain: (e.g. youtube.com, .edu)

Reading Level—This feature allows you to filter search results to match the reading level of your students. You can find results under Basic, Intermediate, or Advanced reading levels. Just click on the appropriate reading level, and the search results will immediately filter out any sites from a different reading level. This would be great to use with your emerging readers in elementary school.

Figure 12.7 Different File Type Filters

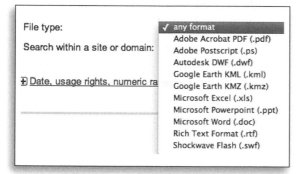

File Type—Another terrific use for Advanced Search is to search for a specific file type. As you know, a standard search in Google provides you with a list of websites that you can use as resources for information. What if you really need a PowerPoint or an Excel spreadsheet, though? It would be almost impossible to search through the pages of results, hoping to find a file amidst the numerous sites—unless, of course, you use Google's Advanced Search to help you find what you're looking for.

Under the File Type, heading you can filter for a specific extension on a file. There are 10 different file types that can serve as filters for your content. Just type in your desired topic, and select the appropriate file type. This is a great way to find a teaching resource, or a form on the district website. For your students, it's a fantastic resource for finding examples of various multimedia projects.

Search Within a Site or Domain—This filter gives you the choice to search for a specific resource on a particular site. You can perform your search on one website versus searching the entire Internet. This can be very helpful when searching on a large site with thousands of possible pages.

After using a few of these Advanced Search techniques, you may never perform a basic Google Search again. Advanced Search isn't a cure-all for your Google queries, but it can dramatically improve your ability to find the right resources on the web.

GOOGLE INSTANT ■

Google Instant is a new way to view your search results while you are typing your search term. In a nutshell, while you start typing a search term, Google Instant will begin to predict your possible searches and instantly show results.

Why Google Instant?

In the world of search results, speed is essential. Google felt that using predictive text and results could save users time in conducting their routine searches. Less time typing and searching means more time learning.

Using Google Instant means you only need an initial idea to begin your search. As soon as you begin typing the letters, Google will share possible conclusions to your search. Since you don't need to finish typing your search term, you'll reach the content more quickly than ever. With Google Instant, you don't even need to hit the Search button!

Now, I know there are those of you out there that want no part of predictive results. If you don't want to use Google Instant, you can always turn it off by following these steps (see Figure 12.8):

1. Go into the **Search Settings** on Google.com.

2. About halfway down the page, you'll find the option, **Do not use Google Instant**. Click the button, and you've disabled Google Instant. You can always turn it on again later.

Figure 12.8　Turning Off Google Instant

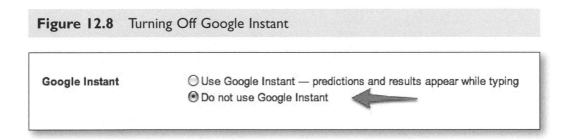

For those of you that like the sound of this searching tool, here is what's in it for you and your students:

- **Faster Searches:** By predicting your search and showing results before you finish typing, Google Instant can save 2–5 seconds per search. Imagine how much time the average student can save on one research project!
- **Smarter Predictions:** Even when you don't know exactly what you're looking for, predictions help guide your search. The top prediction is

shown in grey text, directly in the search box, so you can stop typing as soon as you see what you need.

- **Instant Results:** Start typing, and results appear right before your eyes. Until now, you had to type a full search term, hit return, and hope for the right results. Now results appear instantly as you type, helping you see where you're headed, every step of the way. (www.google.com/insidesearch/instant-about.html)

■ TIMELINE

The first Search tool we'll explore is the Timeline. When you type in a search term with the Timeline, it will provide you with a historical reference to your topic. You'll find this search can be incredibly useful in studying history and social studies (see Figure 12.9).

Figure 12.9   Google Timeline Provides Historical Context for Data

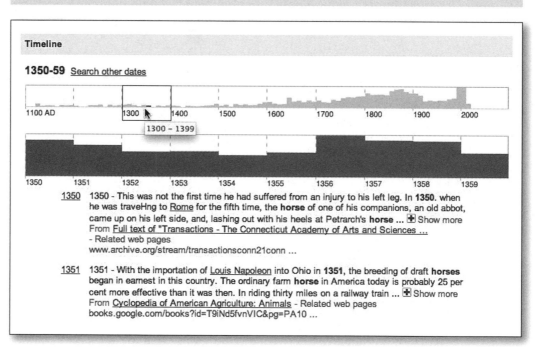

Using the Timeline

- You'll find the **Timeline** along the lower left side of your search results screen in Google.
- When you conduct a search using Timeline, the top of your search results will display a timeline showing the relevant years for that topic.
- You can click on a specific time frame to see results from that period.
- Below the timeline, you'll find search results that describe events contained within the period of time.
- Click on the specific event, and you'll find out more information from the source's website.

Timeline is a great resource for looking at information within the context of time. For some subjects, this will prove to be an essential way to process the information. Google's Timeline is another option for bringing information to your students.

GOOGLE IMAGE SEARCH ■

Google Image Search is both a blessing and a curse for education. It is a huge benefit to your classroom because Image Search can help you and your students find an enormous amount of visual content from the web. You can find pictures to illustrate concepts in a report or presentation. It's amazing the power that an image can have in developing content knowledge. After all, it is no surprise that a picture is said to be worth a thousand words.

But then there's the curse of Google Image Search. Because Google's search engine looks at everything on the web, it can be difficult to filter out inappropriate content. By default, Google is only searching for the term you or your student typed; it isn't trying to determine the appropriateness of the images themselves.

Another big issue with Google Image Search is copyright. Just because Google helped you find a series of images doesn't mean you have permission to use them. Remember, all the images that Google locates in its searches are already on the Web; someone put those images on a website, and Google found them. Before your students use the pictures in a project, in many cases you still need to get permission from the original owner.

In spite of the issues surrounding Google Image Search, it is a wonderful tool, and it can help your students see information in many new ways. Let's take a closer look at how to use the tool.

Finding and Saving an Image

To find and save an image using Google Images, do the following (see Figure 12.10):

1. Go to google.com and click on the **Images** link in the top left corner of your screen.

2. Type your search term in the Google Search box.

3. Your results will come back as a giant grid of images. Hover your mouse over a specific image, and you'll receive additional information about the picture.

4. To save a particular image, double click on the thumbnail version. The image will display in its own window.

5. Right click on the image and choose **Save Image As** from the menu on the screen.

Figure 12.10   Saving an Image From Google Images

Figure 12.11 Filtering in Google Images

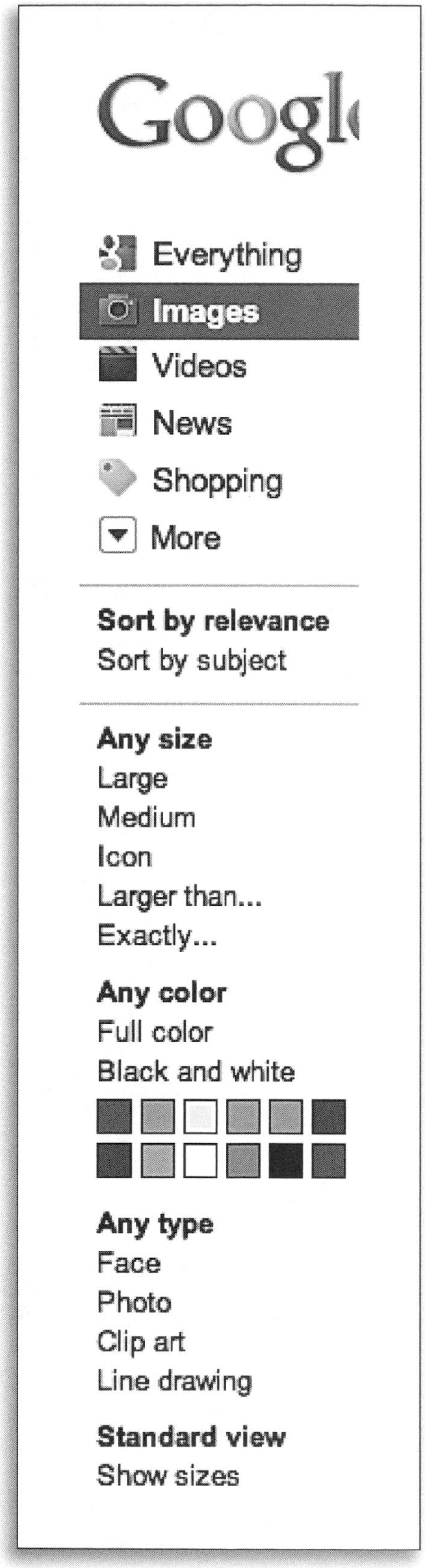

Everything

Images

Videos

News

Shopping

More

Sort by relevance
Sort by subject

Any size
Large
Medium
Icon
Larger than...
Exactly...

Any color
Full color
Black and white

Any type
Face
Photo
Clip art
Line drawing

Standard view
Show sizes

Additional Search Options in Google Images

Besides saving images, there are a variety of filters in the Google Images search function that can help you find and use the images you're looking for in the database.

Sorting by Relevance—Use the **Sort by relevance** option to organize your results by subject. Instead of looking through hundreds of unrelated images, you can see images arranged by a similar feature. Type "mountains" into the Images search box, and you'll find that several categories of mountains are available for viewing. When you click on the **Sort** option, the mountains will be arranged based upon their category.

Image Size—You can filter image results by their size (Click **Any size** at any time to get back to unfiltered results.):

Use these options if you want to see results for a specific range of sizes.

- Click **Medium** to find images with resolutions between 400×300 pixels and 1024×768 pixels.
- Click **Large** to find images with resolutions bigger than 1024×768 pixels.
- Click **Icon** to find square images with the following resolutions: 50×50, 64×64, 96×96, 128×128, and 256×256.

It will also show you images with widths and heights less than or equal to 50 pixels.

For most pictures, you'll want to look at the largest size possible. Why? Once you download an image, you can always resize it to be smaller if necessary. However, if you download a small version of an image, you may not be able to increase the size without "pixelating" it, which distorts the image.

Color—You can filter results by color (Click **Any color** at any time to get back to unfiltered results.):

- Choose **Full color** to see the greatest number of photos available. However, you can filter for **Black and white** if you only want to see those types of images.
- Click a colored square under the **Specific color** link to find images containing that particular color. For our earlier example of mountains, clicking on either **red** or **orange** will result in many of your images having a desert or red rock mountain landscape.

Type—The second group of links filters results by their type. Google Images can automatically detect whether an image is a face, a photograph, clip art, or a line drawing. (Click **Any type** at any time to get back to unfiltered results.)

Show Sizes—Use this option to see each image's size displayed directly on the results page, making it easy to find an image of a specific size.

SAFESEARCH: PROTECTING STUDENTS ■ FROM INAPPROPRIATE IMAGES

I mentioned earlier that a big concern of many teacher and parents is students being exposed to inappropriate pictures in Google Images. The Google Images search lets you search with a filter called SafeSearch, which should keep adult images out of your results (see Figure 12.12). The default is a moderate filter setting, but you can change that by doing the following:

1. Click on the SafeSearch preferences on the right side of the screen on your Google Images results page.

2. In the drop-down menu, select the level of filter you'd like to enable. There are three levels of filtering to choose from: **Off,** meaning no filtering is taking place; **Moderate,** which removes adult images from the search; and **Strict,** which removes all adult images and provides a block against future searches. Strict filtering is most often used by schools.

Figure 12.12 Using Google SafeSearch

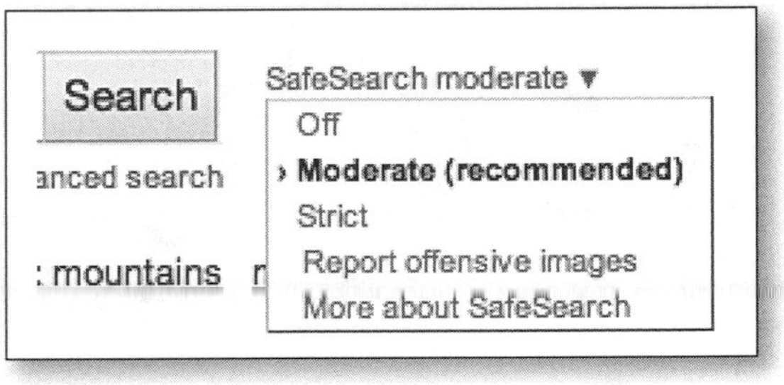

3. The settings will be immediately changed to your chosen selection.

4. You can **Lock** your SafeSearch preferences by going to your Google account settings. Click on the **More about SafeSearch** link in the drop-down menu to get more information.

GOOGLE BOOK SEARCH ■

So far, we've looked at many different ways Google can be used to search for information. One of the key educational sources of information for our students is that of books. For most of us, books were the only way we could conduct research when we were in school. Today, books are still valuable resources for information, but now there's a new way to find them.

Google is committed to creating digital copies of books and storing them within the Google databases. These books are free for you to access and read online. Finding them is as easy as searching for other content with Google. Here's how it works:

1. Go to google.com and click on the **More** link on the menu across the top of the screen.

2. In the drop-down menu, select the **Books** link.

3. The Google Books entry page will display. Here, you can search for books by typing in a keyword, title, author, or line from a specific book.

4. Click on a book title, and you'll see basic info about the book just like you'd see in a card catalog. You might also see a few snippets from books—sentences that use your search term in context.

5. If a publisher or author has given Google permission, you'll see a full page from the book and be able to browse within the book to see more pages. If the book is out of copyright, meaning the book is now in the public domain, you'll see a full page, and you can page forward or back to see the full book.

6. Clicking on **Search within this book** allows you to perform more searches within the book you've selected.

7. Last, you can add the book to a digital library within Google Books, so you can always go back to the book again later.

Google Books is an ambitious project, but its impact can and will be felt by schools for years to come. Who knows? There may be a day where the classroom is full of books, but the shelves are all empty.

■ GOOGLE'S TIME-SAVING SEARCHES

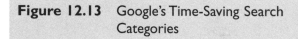

Figure 12.13 Google's Time-Saving Search Categories

Google has limitless amounts of information to search through. At times, it can seem overwhelming. To make the information more manageable, Google has provided some ready-reference categories of basic information that you can search with your students (see Figure 12.13). You can find the entire list at www.google.com/landing/searchtips/

The advantage to using these "time savers" is that your students can find this information quickly, and much of the data is updated in real time. To try any of these searches, go to Google. com and use the search box. Let's look more closely at a few of these search tips.

Weather: When you type "weather" and the name of a city or zip code in the Google Search box, Google will immediately load a 4-day forecast for that spot. You'll also get the current conditions for that location. This information would be great for studying the weather in a science class or as part of an elementary weather unit. (Another Google tip is to add the weather gadget to your iGoogle page so you can always have a forecast on your homepage.)
Example search: weather 90210

Unit Conversion: You can use the unit conversion search to make quick reference to a variety of measurements. You can convert distances, weights, volumes, and more to help your students understand the different units of measurement. Just type the desired conversion, and let Google take care of the rest.

Example search: 2,000 feet in miles

Dictionary: Google can help your students find definitions for unknown words. Just type "define" along with the word, and Google will search the web for a list of definitions. Along with the definitions is a reference to the site that provided the information.

Example search: define education

Calculator: One of the hidden gems in Google Search is a built-in calculator. Now, you might think that this calculator can only perform basic functions like addition, subtraction, multiplication, and division, but it can handle so much more. Google Calculator can perform operations such as tangents, sine, percentages, and so on. The hardest part of using Google Calculator is knowing how to type the equations. If you can type it, Google can solve it.

Example calculation: 5*9+(sqrt 10)^3=

Fill in the Blank: How many times have you gone to Google to search for the answer to a specific question? Fill in the Blank is the answer to your search needs. Type your statement and put an asterisk in the blank part of your query. The search results will return with your answer bolded in the site descriptions.

Example search: Cheese is made of *

Public Data: This search provides you with information about recent trends in population and unemployment rates across the United States. Type your desired search, either population or unemployment, and then the state for which you'd like the data. Google will provide you with a graph summarizing recent trends for that data search (see Figure 12.14). This could be used in a geography or business class when looking for current information and trends.

Example search: population Wyoming

Figure 12.14   Track Population Data With Public Data

GOOGLE TRANSLATE ■

Google's databases contain dozens of different languages from which to search. With so many languages at its disposal, it begs the question, why can't Google simply translate text from one language to another? Ask no more; let's look at Google Translate (see Figure 12.15).

Figure 12.15   Google Translate Interface

To translate words and phrases, simply select your translation languages and start typing. The translation result should appear instantly as you type, without your having to click a single button. Or, you can always click the **Translate** button to trigger a translation.

When you translate a single word, you may see a simple dictionary at the bottom of the page indicating parts of speech and possible word variations. Be sure to check for multiple definitions, as the first definition may not be the most common.

For most translations, you can also access a **View Detailed Dictionary** link. This will display a more detailed Google Dictionary page with example sentences, images, and more.

If you aren't sure what language you're attempting to translate, the **Detect language option** can figure this out for you. The accuracy of the automatic language detection increases with the amount of text entered, so as you keep typing in Google Translate, it gets better at recognizing words and phrases.

Translate Webpages

One of the best features in Google Translate is the ability to translate an entire webpage.

- To complete the translation, simply enter the webpage's address (e.g., www.uen.org) into the input box and click **Translate**.
- Instantly, your webpage will transition from English to your language of choice. What a tremendous option to help our ESL students in their new classrooms!

If you hover your mouse over the translated text, the original text for the highlighted segment is displayed in an info bubble just above the translated text. To see all of the original text of the page, click the **View: Original** radio button in the top frame of the translated page.

Translate Documents From Your Computer

Google Translate also provides an easy way to translate whole documents, without the need for copying and pasting large blocks of text. Simply click the **translate a document** link and submit your file as a PDF, TXT, DOC, PPT, XLS, or RTF. In just a few moments, your document will display in Google Docs in the new language.

Please note that the translation may not always be in the most conversational language. Google Translate has been known to present a fairly literal translation, which gets the meaning across, even if it uses words or phrases that some native speakers would not typically use in conversation.

Project Idea: Using Google Translate in Your Classroom

Imagine having a built-in translator available 24/7 for use with your students. Here are some possible ideas for its use:

- **Dictionary for Foreign Language Students**—Rather than buying an expensive dictionary, have your foreign language students use Google Translate to help them with basic vocabulary. The students can work in both languages to ensure they are using words and phrases correctly. As a quick assessment tool, Google Translate can help kids know if they are learning the right words.

- **Pen Pals With Foreign Students**—Using Google Translate, you can have e-mail communication with students from different countries. Gmail can automatically translate the messages from the students. Students in the foreign country will have your students' messages in their native tongue. The messages your students receive can be read in English. What a great way to bring the world's students together!

> **NETS-S Standard 2 Objective c**
>
> Students use digital media and environments to communicate and work collaboratively, including at a distance, to support individual learning and contribute to the learning of others. Students develop cultural understanding and global awareness by engaging with learners of other cultures. (ISTE, 2007)

- **Translate School Documents for Parents**—Be sure to have copies of the important classroom documents available in the languages your students' parents speak. Using the Translate Document feature, you can have your files available for everyone. Even better, you can show parents how they can use Google Translate at home so they can get copies of every document they need to read. This is a great way to include ESL students and their parents in your classes. It builds a sense of community and lets every voice be heard.

MORE IDEAS FOR GOING GOOGLE

- Now that you've learned some new search techniques, try making another search story. By using better searching tools, your students can really tell some interesting stories.
- You can use all of these search techniques on a mobile device. Even if students don't have a smart phone, they can text Google to receive search results. Text to Google (466453) with your desired search, and you'll get the answers in return. This works for any of the time savers that were discussed in this chapter.

TIPS FOR THE GOOGLE CLASSROOM

- Try using Google Chrome as your default browser. One of my favorite features is the built-in search in the address bar. Instead of going to Google.com to create a search, simply type right in the address bar, and you'll get the search results you desire.
- Another reason to try Google Chrome is that it allows you to sync your browsers at home and work. When you use Google Chrome on two different computers, you can have the bookmarks and other browser settings sync to both machines. This means a link you bookmark at home will exist on your computer at work. To set up sync, you'll need to go to the options menu (PC) or the preferences menu (Mac).

13

Google Custom Search

Before we leave the topic of searching, one last tool we need to address is Google Custom Search. What is it? With Custom Search, educators can create a filtered search on a specific group of pages. For example, rather than having my students conduct a search on Martin Luther King, Jr., on the entire web, I can create a search engine for some specific sites that provide quality information about Dr. King. This means my students aren't exposed to resources that aren't valid and may contain questionable materials. As the teacher, I control which sites are included in the search, so I can help determine which sites my students are exposed to.

> **NETS-T Standard 3 Objective d**
>
> Teachers exhibit knowledge, skills, and work processes representative of an innovative professional in a global and digital society. Teachers model and facilitate effective use of current and emerging digital tools to locate, analyze, evaluate, and use information resources to support research and learning. (ISTE, 2008)

HOW TO SET UP A CUSTOM SEARCH ■

To set up a Custom Search, go to www.google.com/cse and click on **Create a Custom Search Engine.** You can then configure your search in three steps (see Figure 13.1):

1. Set up your search by

    a. Providing the **Name** of the search.

    b. Giving a **Description** of the search or topic.

    c. Defining your search engine: Include the desired sites for the search. Just add one URL to each line in the search box.

    d. Choosing the **Standard edition** for the search. This is a free search you can use with your students.

    e. Agreeing to the terms and clicking **Next**.

Figure 13.1 Setting up a Custom Search Engine

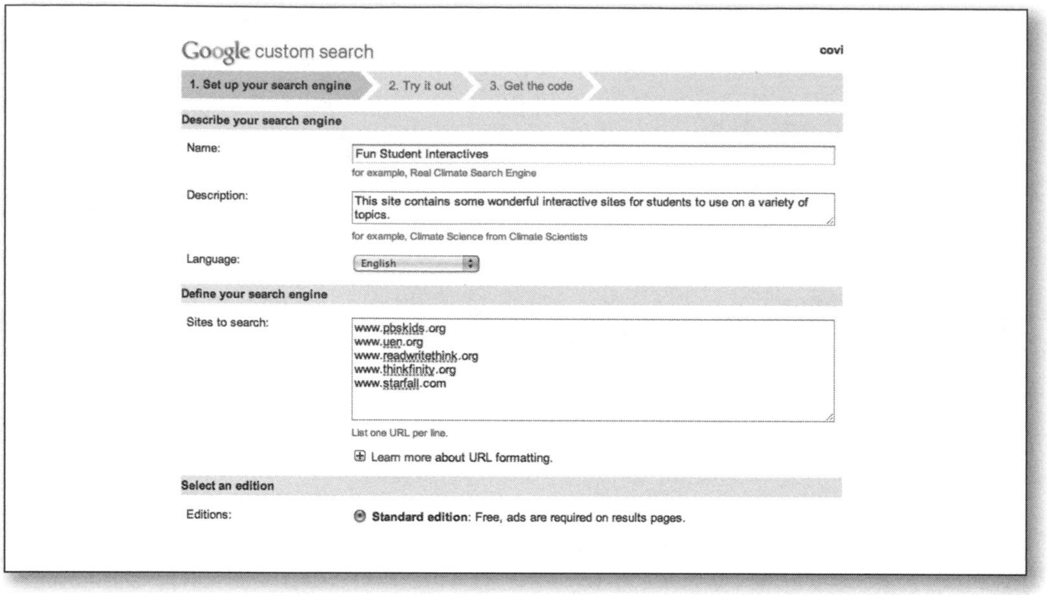

2. The second step in setting up your Customized Search Engine is to **Try it Out:**

   a. Choose the **template** layout for your search results. There are a few different options for you.

   b. **Test your search** engine by typing a possible search in the provided window and previewing the results.

   c. If you're satisfied with the search results, click **Next;** if not, click **Back,** and include some different websites in your search.

3. Once you've created the Custom Search Engine, Google will provide you with the HTML code to add the search box to your website. If you don't have a website, Google will host your results for you.

   a. At the top of the page, click on the **Look and Feel** link.

   b. You'll be prompted to choose a hosting option. The final choice is a **Google-hosted page.**

   c. Click on the **Save** option.

■ SHARING YOUR CUSTOM SEARCH WITH STUDENTS

- Sharing your Custom Search with students requires a final step (see Figure 13.2).
- While in the editing mode, you can choose your custom search from along the left side of the screen.
- You'll find it under the **My Search Engines** link.
- You can also find and manage your Search Engines from www.google.com/cse. Just click the link for **Manage your existing search engines.**

Figure 13.2 Share Your Custom Search

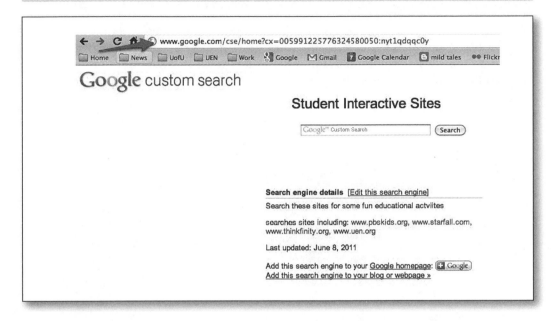

Figure 13.3 Manage Your Custom Search

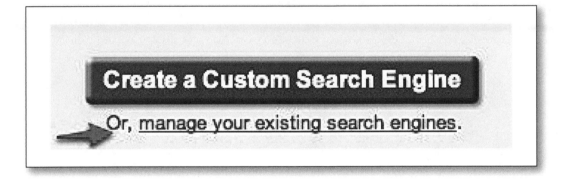

- Choose your search engine from the list that displays on the screen.
- Copy the link in the URL window, and provide this to your students.
- All the search results will come from your Custom Search Engine and the sites you selected to include.

Google Custom Search Engine is incredibly useful for teachers. Essentially, you create your own search engine by selecting the sites that Google will index. It searches only the sites I specify, bypassing a lot of the junk. (Nate Grondin, social studies teacher, as quoted in Google, 2011b, n.p.)

Using Google Custom Search is a nice alternative to costly filtering and unsupervised searching. For younger grades, it's a great way for teachers to help students learn the power of searching, while providing them with a productive and safe environment.

MORE IDEAS FOR GOING GOOGLE

- You can have your students create a custom search engine as part of a research project they develop. This is an interesting way for students to find useful sites and share them with other members of class. An activity like this will help students think critically and evaluate web resources.

TIPS FOR THE GOOGLE CLASSROOM

- You can embed your Google Custom Search Engine on your classroom or school website. When you are in the Manage Your Site mode, look under the Control Panel menus (down the left side of the screen) for Get Code. This option will provide you with the HTML code you can use to embed the custom search on a website.

14

Information With Google

❧❧

FIVE THINGS TO KNOW ABOUT INFORMATION WITH GOOGLE

1. Google Alerts lets you subscribe to e-mail summaries of news and information.
2. Google Reader provides a one-stop site to read web content.
3. Using Reader, you can subscribe to blogs, news feeds, and more.
4. iGoogle transforms Google.com into your own personal information source.
5. iGoogle can be customized so the theme reflects your interests.

❧❧

Getting information is more important than ever, or at least it seems that way because there is more information available than ever before. With Google tools, you have so many different ways to access data on the web to help you and your students digest the world around you.

In the next few chapters, we're going to focus on a few tools that can help you find current information and manage the content you're interested in. Specifically, we'll explore Google Alerts, Google Reader, and iGoogle. Each of these sites can help you find information and store it in a central location. With these Google tools, you can bring the web to you, rather than spending your time searching the web.

> ### NETS-S Standard 3 Objective c
>
> Students apply digital tools to gather, evaluate, and use information. Students evaluate and select information sources and digital tools based on the appropriateness to specific tasks. (ISTE, 2007)

15

Google Alerts

Teachers seem to love using Google as a search engine to help them, as well as their students, research a variety of subjects. As teachers conduct these Google searches, one of the biggest challenges they face is trying to find the latest research on topics for their class. There is so much information, and no one has the time to sort through the endless amounts of material.

What if there was a way that Google could help you by sorting through the vast quantity of information on the Internet? Enter Google Alerts—it finds the best material from the web and sends you links to it on a regularly scheduled basis. It's a great way for you and your students to conduct research without needing to spend hours searching the Internet.

> **NETS-T Standard 3 and Objective c**
>
> Teachers exhibit knowledge, skills, and work processes representative of an innovative professional in a global and digital society. Teachers communicate relevant information and ideas effectively to students, parents, and peers using a variety of digital-age media and formats. (ISTE, 2008)

WHAT ARE GOOGLE ALERTS? ■

Google Alerts are compiled lists of articles and websites, sent to you in the form of e-mails when Google finds new results—such as web pages, newspaper articles, or blogs—that match your search term. You can use Google Alerts to monitor anything on the web. For your next classroom research project, imagine having Google search for the latest information on the Web. This is basically how it works:

1. Enter a query in Google Alerts that you're researching.

2. Google Alerts checks on a scheduled basis to see if there are new results for your query.

3. When there are new results, Google Alerts sends you an e-mail with the new information.

■ USING GOOGLE ALERTS

To use Google Alerts, do the following (see Figure 15.1):

Figure 15.1 Using Google Alerts

1. Go to alerts.google.com.

2. Enter your query. It works just the same as a normal Google search. You can use multiple search terms, or identify specific query modifiers for your search.

3. You can preview your search results to get a sense of the information that pertains to your query.

4. Select the **Type** of search results you want. Choose from News, Blogs, Discussions, Video, and more.

5. Choose how often you want to receive the alerts. You can select from the following options:

    a. **As it Happens:** This is the fastest return of results, but you will likely receive a large amount of material. For a popular topic, you'll receive a constant stream of e-mails.

    b. **Once a Day:** This is the default setting for Google Alerts. On a daily basis, you'll receive a compiled list of the relevant search results.

    c. **Once a Week:** Every week, you'll be e-mailed a list of the compiled search results.

6. Select the **Volume** of your search results. You can choose to receive all the possible search results, or you can have Google send you **Only the best results.**

7. Enter the e-mail address to which you want your alerts delivered. I'd naturally suggest you choose your Gmail address, but it's not a requirement.

8. If you aren't signed in to your account, Google will send you a confirmation e-mail to validate your new alert. If you are signed in to a Google account when you create an alert, you don't need to confirm it.

That's it! Your alert is now active. From this point forward, you'll receive an e-mail whenever Google Alerts finds new results for your search.

You can manage your alert in each e-mail message (see Figure 15.2). Also, each e-mail you receive contains a link to delete the alert, so you can cancel any time you want.

Google Alerts Tips

- Try to be as precise as possible. The more precise your search terms are, the more relevant your alerts will be.
- Use quotes around words if you are looking for them together.
- Examples:

   o "white house"
   o "Barack Obama"

- Use a minus sign (-) in front of words that you want to exclude.
- Examples:

   o paris -texas
   o apple -fruit

- Put a plus sign (+) immediately before a word to match that word precisely as you typed it, excluding synonyms and spelling variations.
- Examples:

   o +ford (to stop Google including results for Ford)
   o Michael +Jackson (to stop Google including results for Michael Jackson)

- Use the site: operator to limit your search to specific sites.
- Examples:

   o physics site:.edu
   o congress site:nytimes.com

- Use the site: operator with a dash to exclude specific sites.
- Example:

   o "joebloggs" -site:twitter.com (Google, 2011f, n.p.)

Figure 15.2 Manage Google Alerts From Your E-mail

Remove this alert.
Create another alert.
Manage your alerts.

For your next research project, have your students set up Google Alerts to help them find the most current information. While you're at it, using Google Alerts can help you find the materials you may need to supplement your lessons or research as well.

MORE IDEAS FOR GOING GOOGLE

- Teach a lesson on safe practices on the Web by having your students create an alert on themselves. This is a good way to see what is being said about you on the Internet.
- Have students create a keyword alert that tracks their school or the district as a class project to find what information is being published to the Web.

TIPS FOR THE GOOGLE CLASSROOM

A great way to organize your Google Alerts is to create a filter in your Gmail inbox (see Figure 15.3). This means all the alerts for a specific topic will filter directly into a folder, rather than cluttering up your inbox. If you're working on a lengthy research project, the Alerts e-mails can become a bit overwhelming if you don't have a plan for organizing them. Here's how to set it up, if you're using Gmail:

1. Click on the **Settings** icon in the top right corner of the screen.

2. Choose **Mail settings** from the drop-down menu.

3. Select **Filters** from the menu within the Settings tab.

4. Click the **Create a new filter** link at the bottom of the window.

5. This menu gives you several choices for how to filter your messages. I find the easiest way to filter is by keyword using the **Has the words** field.

6. Click the **Next** button.

7. Now you want to determine the effect of the filter. Generally, I find I want to accomplish two things with the filter

   a. **Skip the Inbox** with Alerts so they don't go to the inbox.

   b. Move the alerts inside their own folder by **Applying a new label.**

Figure 15.3   Creating a Filter in Gmail

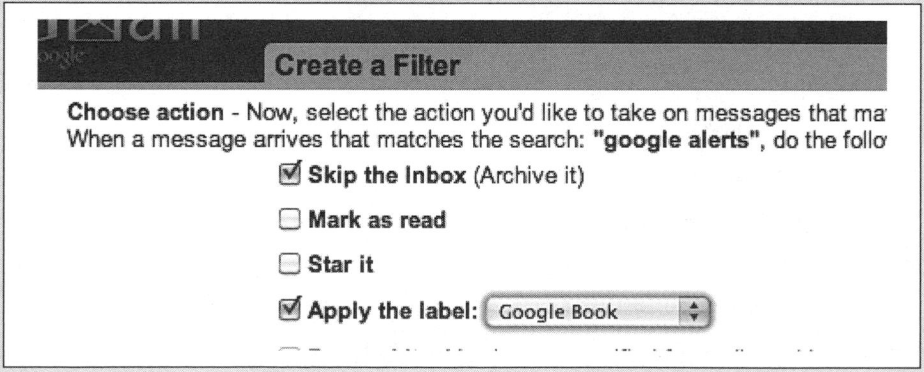

8. Once you've checked the appropriate boxes, click the **Create Filter** button. You're done!

16

Google Reader

Google Reader is an aggregating tool for gathering, reading, and sharing all the different blogs and websites you read on the web. Basically, the idea is that rather than your going to several different websites and blogs every day. Google Reader will find any new content on those sites and blogs and bring it to you. For teachers and students, this can save time by allowing you to ignore sites without new content so you can only read the new information you're interested in. It's all going to be found in one location, so you can find everything you need without spending a lot of time searching. So, how does Google Reader work? It starts with something simple—RSS.

NETS-T Standard 3 Objective d

Teachers exhibit knowledge, skills, and work processes representative of an innovative professional in a global and digital society. Teachers model and facilitate effective use of current and emerging digital tools to locate, analyze, evaluate, and use information resources to support research and learning. (ISTE, 2008)

WHAT'S AN RSS FEED? ■

RSS stands for Really Simple Syndication. RSS feeds are a way for websites to distribute new content as it becomes available.

An RSS feed functions as a file that contains a blog or website's most recent entries. When you subscribe to a site's feed in Reader, you will automatically be notified when that website contains new posts or entries. Instead of your having to check sites repeatedly for updates, RSS feeds bring your favorite websites to you! This saves you time and makes you more effective in searching for the content you're interested in.

Imagine that every new post you write on your classroom blog is immediately sent to the Google Reader account of every one of the parents and students. A good marketing plan for your classroom has to include ways to get your information out to your audience—rather than bringing your parents to your blog, Google Reader can bring your blog to them!

An RSS feed can be identified by this universal symbol. When you see it on a website, clicking will usually direct you to that site's feed. From there, you can either copy and paste the link to subscribe to the feed in Google Reader, or in the case of many browsers, click a button to subscribe directly.

You should be aware that not all websites contain an RSS feed on their main page. You may have to search for the term RSS along the menus on the site. If there isn't an RSS feed available, it is usually due to the fact that there isn't regularly updated information on the website.

Typically, blogs will have an RSS feed, as that is one of the big features of blogging—content is updated frequently. Whenever a new post is written, the RSS feed will bring the content to your Google Reader account.

Subscribe to a Feed

For most blogs, the site will automatically tell Reader where to find a blog's feed. If this doesn't work, you'll have to add the URL of a site's feed directly. Find the RSS logo on the site in question, click it, and copy and paste the link into the "add subscription" box. If you can't find an RSS logo on the site, the site may not offer RSS feeds. When you click on many RSS feed links, you'll be taken to a webpage that contains a lot of HTML code. Don't worry about this. If the RSS link doesn't appear directly, copy the URL from the address window of your browser.

To subscribe to a feed in Reader,

SUBSCRIBE

1. Click the **Subscribe** button in your left-hand sidebar.

2. Enter the URL of the blog or site you'd like to subscribe to.

3. Click **Add.**

The site will appear at the bottom of your list of feeds.

Organize Your Feeds

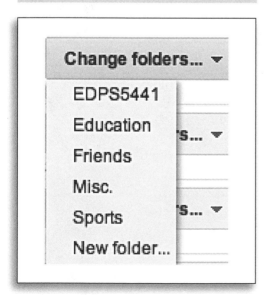

Figure 16.1 Create a New Folder

Once you get a few feeds into Google Reader, a good idea for managing your sites is to create collections of similar topics using folders (see Figure 16.1). For example, if I was an elementary teacher and followed blogs from various curriculums, I would keep all of my Math feeds separate from my Language Arts feeds. Here's how to do this:

1. Click on the **Manage Subscriptions** link. It's located at the bottom of your list of feeds.

2. Select the **Change Folder** button.

3. In the drop-down menu, choose **New Folder.**

4. The new folder will display at the top of your list of feeds. Drag the appropriate feed(s) into the new folder.

5. Repeat as necessary.

Reading Feeds

Once you've subscribed feeds from blogs or websites and organized them into folders, it's time to read new content (see Figure 16.2).

Figure 16.2 Reading a Post in Google Reader

You'll see the number of new or unread items in parentheses next to the website or blog's title. When you click on the title, Google Reader will display the contents of the feed in your primary window.

Figure 16.3 Settings Icon in Google Reader

- You can choose to view all items or just new items.
- As you scroll past items in a feed, those items will be marked as read, and more items will automatically appear.
- You can toggle this by clicking on the **Settings** link at the top right-hand corner of your Reader window (see Figure 16.3).
- Next, uncheck the **Scroll Tracking** checkbox. This means that articles will be marked as "read" just by scrolling through them.
- If you'd just like to browse headlines, click **List View** in the top right-hand corner of the main Reader window.
- You can then click on an individual item in List View to expand it.
- Click on **Expanded View** to return to the default view where each item is already expanded.

Figure 16.4 Expanded View Option

So, why use Google Reader? It saves you time in reading the latest information from your Personal Learning Network. Because all the new content is highlighted and stored in one location, you can quickly access the information and move on.

MORE IDEAS FOR GOING GOOGLE

- If you create a class blog, be sure to embed the Add to Google button on your site. This button allows a reader to automatically subscribe to your content through an RSS feed in Google Reader. You can find a simple wizard to create the button and get the HTML code to embed on your blog on this site: www.google.com/webmasters/add.html.

TIPS FOR THE GOOGLE CLASSROOM

Figure 16.5   Use the Google Reader Gadget on iGoogle

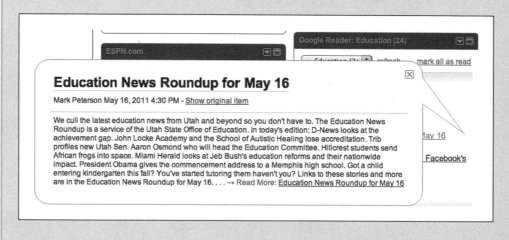

- Use the iGoogle Gadget for Google Reader: In the next chapter, you'll learn about iGoogle as a way to customize your Google homepage.
- One of the gadgets you can add allows you to get your Google Reader feeds sent directly to your iGoogle page (see Figure 16.5). This is another way to save time and keep in touch with the latest information from your favorite blogs and other RSS feeds.

17
iGoogle

Google's homepage is one of the most recognized sites on the web. Due to its simple features, powerful search results, and clean look, it is also one of the easiest sites to use. But Google can do more than just search; with your Google account, you can choose to customize your Google homepage. This new customized homepage is called iGoogle, and it may change the way you look at Google (see Figure 17.1 on the following page).

iGoogle allows you to add RSS feeds and content gadgets to your Google homepage. This can become your main entry page into all of the different Google tools. In addition, you can create customized gadgets that contain information that is important for you and your students.

NETS-T Standard 3 Objective d

Teachers exhibit knowledge, skills, and work processes representative of an innovative professional in a global and digital society. Teachers model and facilitate effective use of current and emerging digital tools to locate, analyze, evaluate, and use information resources to support research and learning. (ISTE, 2008)

GETTING STARTED IN IGOOGLE ■

Setting up your iGoogle page takes only a few minutes, but you need to know how to switch from Google's Classic homepage to your new iGoogle page. Here's how to get started:

1. Go to google.com.

2. Next to the login, you'll find the **Settings** icon (it looks like a gear—see Figure 17.2 on the following page). Click on the gear, and you'll find iGoogle in the drop-down menu.

3. At the bottom right, click **sign in.** Once you've logged in, you'll find that your Google homepage has changed. Instead of just seeing the basic Google search box, you'll find the search field.

4. You'll be prompted to add different content fields and/or websites.

5. Click **Save.**

Figure 17.1   iGoogle Customized Layout

Figure 17.2   Accessing iGoogle From the Settings Icon

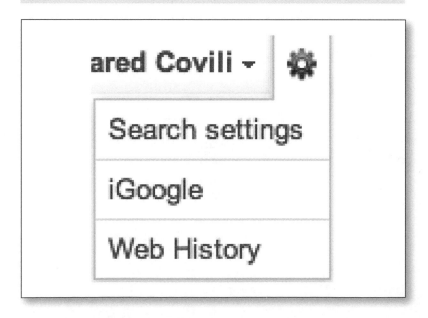

On your initial visit to iGoogle, you'll start customizing your page by selecting some of the sites and categories you're most interested in. Be sure you save the choices you've made, and you'll be ready to access the content (see Figure 17.3).

Figure 17.3 Initial Setup of iGoogle Page

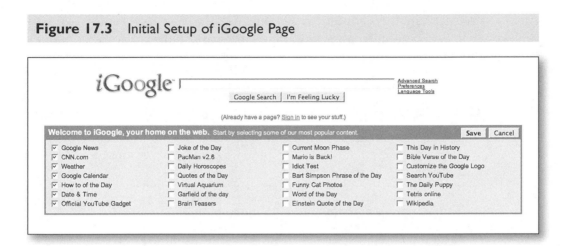

CUSTOMIZING THE THEME ■ OF YOUR IGOOGLE PAGE

One of the fun aspects of your iGoogle page is that you can add a favorite header image and background theme. There are tons of them to choose from.

1. In the bottom right corner of your current iGoogle banner, click either **Add gadgets** or **Change theme,** and you'll find all kinds of choices.

2. Browse through the various themes and when you find one you like, click on the **Add** button.

You can change your theme at any time. Just repeat the process.

ADDING GADGETS TO YOUR PAGE ■

The biggest reason to create an iGoogle page is to customize the site with the different content you're interested in on the web. Let's look at adding gadgets to your iGoogle page.

1. As with themes, click on the **Add gadgets** link in the bottom right corner of your iGoogle banner.

2. Choose the **Gadgets** tab. You'll find several categories of gadgets along the left side of the screen.

3. You can also **Search** for a gadget using the window along the top right side of the current screen.

4. When you find your desired gadget, preview it by clicking on its name or **Add it now** using that button.

5. Select the **Back to iGoogle** home link where you'll find your newly added gadget along the top left side of your iGoogle homepage.

Adding Gadgets Using RSS Feeds

Another way to add gadgets to your iGoogle page is through an RSS feed. As we discussed in the chapter on Google Reader, RSS feeds allow you to receive updated content on a variety of websites and blogs. Adding a gadget from an RSS feed requires two steps:

Figure 17.4   Adding an RSS Feed

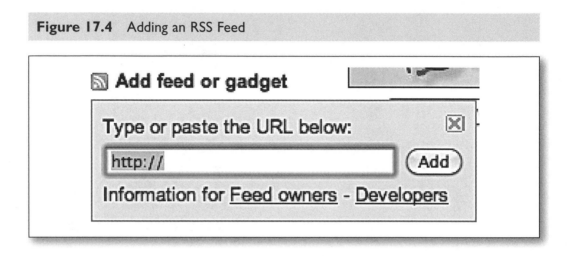

1. Find and copy the URL for the website you'd like to turn into a gadget.

2. Paste the URL of the website into the provided window and click **Add.**

If there is an RSS feed available on the site or blog, the gadget will be created and added to your iGoogle page. If there isn't a feed present on the site, there will be a message letting you know that the gadget wasn't created.

■ EDITING AND MOVING GADGETS

Figure 17.5   Edit Your Gadgets in iGoogle

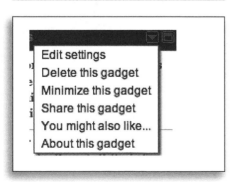

When you add a new gadget to your iGoogle page, it comes with default settings. In order for you to use it effectively. you'll want to edit the settings for your personal preferences. Also, gadgets can be moved around, so you can customize the layout of your iGoogle page.

• In the top right corner of each iGoogle gadget, you'll find a drop-down menu that provides you with **Editing** controls.
• Each gadget's controls will differ, but many will require that you enter a username and password if accessing your personal account.

- You can **Delete** any gadget using that link in the menu.
- Also, sharing a gadget is simple. Just click on the **Share this gadget** link and type the e-mail address of your desired recipient.

Once you have your gadgets set up correctly, you can move them around on your page by moving your cursor along the title bar of the banner. Your cursor will turn into a four-pronged arrow. Left click on the gadget, and drag it into your desired position.

Project Idea: Creating and Sharing a New Tab With Students

iGoogle is a terrific tool for teachers to find and use information. The problem is that you're the only one who can access that content. But Google has a solution to this dilemma. You can create additional tabs for your iGoogle page that can be shared with your students. Imagine finding several resources in iGoogle that could help students with an upcoming test. Now you can share those gadgets as a compiled tab that all of your students can access through e-mail. Setting up and sharing a tab is simple. Let's learn how to get it done.

Setting up a new tab is a one-click process. In the top left corner of your iGoogle page is the **Home** tab. It's the default tab in iGoogle, but you can add more tabs that have specific content.

NETS-T Standard 3 and Objective C

Teachers exhibit knowledge, skills, and work processes representative of an innovative professional in a global and digital society. Teachers communicate relevant information and ideas effectively to students, parents, and peers using a variety of digital-age media and formats. (ISTE, 2008)

1. To create a new tab, click the drop-down menu next to the Home tab.

2. Select **Add a tab** from this menu.

3. You'll be prompted to name the new tab (see Figure 17.7). Depending on your choice, iGoogle can actually find gadgets for your new tab based upon the topic of your title. Choose the **I'm Feeling Lucky** option, and iGoogle will autofill your new tab with several topic-related gadgets.

4. The new tab will appear on the left side of your iGoogle screen, below the Home tab.

Figure 17.6 Sharing a Tab in iGoogle

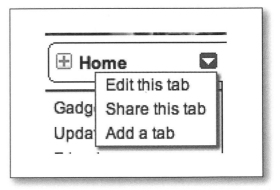

Once you have all the gadgets you want on your new tab, it's time to share it with students.

1. While on your new tab, click on the drop-down menu. Remember, it's located along the left side of the screen.

Figure 17.7 Creating a New Tab

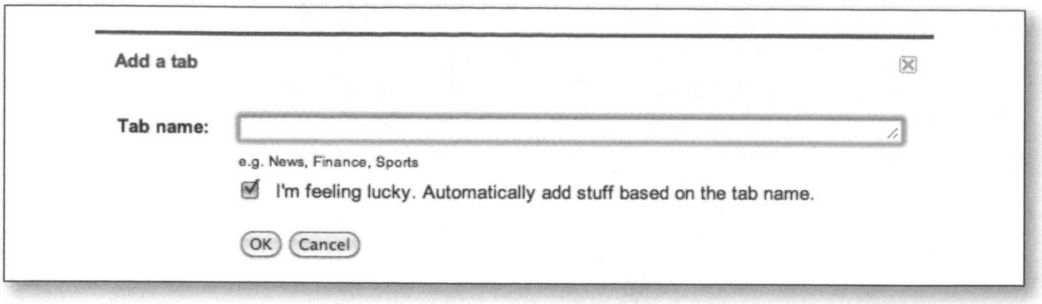

2. Choose **Share this tab.**

3. A window will open that allows you to enter the e-mail addresses of any students with whom you'd like to share this gadget. You can pick and choose which gadgets to include and whether or not to include your customized settings for the gadgets.

4. Your students will receive the e-mail, and they can then add the tab to their personal iGoogle page.

Creating a tab of gadgets is an easy way for you to find quick resources and share them with your students using iGoogle. Since you've already evaluated the resources before you share them, you can feel comfortable with the content of the gadgets students will see, and you can provide equal access to the same information for all your students.

MORE IDEAS FOR GOING GOOGLE

- Student-Created Research Tab of Gadgets in iGoogle—Have your students search for useful gadgets for a specific topic they're studying in class. It's one thing for you, as the teacher, to provide a tab of gadgets for the kids, but it's just as important to have them find and evaluate information they can share with the class.
- Students can create their own tab of gadgets and share them with you as part of their research projects in class. Combined with a summary e-mail or annotated reflection, they can share why they picked certain gadgets and how they feel the gadgets could be part of their research in class.

TIPS FOR THE GOOGLE CLASSROOM

- Be sure to maximize your use of Google tools by using the Google-created gadgets on your iGoogle page.
- Some of the most useful gadgets include Google Calendar, Gmail, Google Reader, and Google Docs. You can have quick access to these tools as part of your iGoogle homepage. This will save you time, as you can find the latest information from each of these tools in one location.

Conclusion

Over the course of this book, we've explored how Google can help the class-room teacher and his or her students achieve 21st century learning skills. With a basic Google account, there is so much your students can accomplish. They can collaborate, create, share, produce, find, develop, and communicate with each other and with the world. It's incredible to consider the power contained within the tools we've discussed in the previous chapters.

Still, there is one key Google feature we have yet to address, and it could be the most important yet in developing a technology implementation strategy in your classroom. Google Apps for Education allows your entire school or district to adopt a suite of Google tools for use with all students and faculty.

WHAT'S INCLUDED IN GOOGLE ■ APPS FOR EDUCATION?

We've explored a dozen Google tools you can use in your classroom, but there are only a few that were important enough to include in Google Apps. This exclusive library of tools includes Gmail, Google Calendar, Google Docs, Google Video, Google Sites, and Google Chat. Your school or district can include additional tools in your version of Google Apps, as there are several more apps, or applications, to choose from.

WHY ADOPT GOOGLE APPS? ■

With Google Apps, you have access to tools that provide your school with a fully supported e-mail system. Your school can have its own video repository that is safe and private, for only your students and faculty. Google Apps provides you with a secure library for all your documents, spreadsheets, and presentations. Best of all, Google Apps is completely free for your school or district!

Imagine all the costs your school would save. Without paying for each of these systems, you can use those funds in other ways. In a time when budgets are tight, this is a huge benefit to your school's bottom line. In addition, here is a quick list of reasons why many schools have chosen to use Google Apps.

1. Students will love you for it—Schools tell us that when they ask their students what e-mail they'd prefer, they overwhelmingly say Gmail.

"Our students approached us about a year ago, saying that we needed to improve our email and collaboration services. We actually had our student government tell us, 'we want you to implement Google Apps.'"—Wendy Woodward, Director of Technology Support Services at Northwestern University.

2. Save money—Outsourcing the maintenance of servers to Google frees up resources that would have been spent on additional licenses and upgrades.

"This helped our IT staff understand that their focus should be on strategic enterprise solutions to help us reach our educational objectives, not just over-seeing commodities like email. Had we not gone with the Google solution, we'd be looking at proposing a significant increase in student fees."—Eric Hawley, Associate Vice President for Technology at Utah State University.

3. Innovation in real time—What better way to prepare your students for the newest technology in the workplace than by giving it to them as a part of their education?

"The response from the university community has been extremely positive because we are now partnering with cutting-edge technologists who under-stand that we're trying to provide the latest, most innovative technologies available today."—Roy B. Roberti, Director of Information Technology Planning, Hofstra University.

4. Collaborate globally—Google Docs doesn't just give students and teachers access to the same document. It actually allows students to work on the same document at the same time from anywhere in the world.

"Constructing lesson plans and unit plans is no longer a solitary activity. It's a collaborative process that's happening not only with teachers on a building level team, but with teachers at a grade level from a variety of schools. Our teaching is made better as a result of this collective intelligence."—John Krouskoff, Director of Technology, Clarkstown Central School District. (Google, 2011d, n.p.)

Google Apps is the primary way in which many schools and districts are implementing an organized approach to technology integration. That being said, it's not the only way to have a Google-assisted classroom. Even if your school or district doesn't choose to adopt Google Apps, you can still incorpo-rate Google Tools in your classroom. Several of the activities in this book don't even require a Google account for students to be successful. As you work with different Google tools, you'll find ways to incorporate technology in your teaching.

Throughout this book, we've explored the impact that Google can have in your daily activities. Using a combination of Google tools can impact sev-eral areas in your classroom. From using Google Calendar to help you orga-nize your lessons and share information about the class schedule with parents and students, to creating innovative multimedia projects with Google Earth, there are so many different ways that Google can complement your teaching practice.

THE CONSTANT OF CHANGE ■

Google has always been known for innovation in their tools. That is wonderful for users, as the products they love keep getting better with each additional feature. The problem comes in trying to use a book like this as a final answer to every question about the tools. Rather than giving you a complete list of all the menus and features for each Google tool, I hope this book has been an example of what is possible when implementing the programs as part of your curriculum.

Even as the tools change, the ideas remain constant. Google Docs will allow your students to collaborate with one another on a variety of documents. Google Earth will provide innovative options for exploring the world and creating your own unique tours of different locations. Google Sites will help you share your classroom events, materials, and information with parents and students. Despite the changing menus and displays, you can feel confident that Google will continue to provide you and your students with the tools you'll need to achieve 21st century skills.

GOING GOOGLE IN THE ■
21ST CENTURY CLASSROOM

Using 21st century skills as the foundation for your curriculum will move you toward technology tools that can positively influence your students' achievement. By using Google tools with your students, you'll find that they can more effectively communicate with the world, they will be able to create projects that illustrate their innovative ideas, and students will become problem solvers—able to think critically about issues and concepts.

At the beginning of this book, I shared the simple message on a bumper sticker—"I've Gone Google." While "going Google" has been interpreted as using Google tools as part of one's everyday workflow, going Google in the 21st century classroom means more than using an Internet search engine. Going Google in the classroom is a commitment to technology integration and 21st century learning skills. It is a desire to use tools to promote collaboration and communication, to develop creativity and innovation, and to strengthen the critical thinking and problem solving abilities of our students.

I hope that this book has provided you with a model of how Google tools can help you in your classroom. Don't be afraid to use Google for much more than a search engine—to truly "go Google." You may be glad you did!

Glossary

Circles: Identifies a group of contacts in Google+. Typically, a circle is created as a way to separate contacts that have a similar relationship to the account owner (e.g., business contacts, friends, etc.).

Cloud computing: Denotes a change in the way documents, images, and data are stored. Rather than storing information on your personal computer's hard drive, the data is uploaded to a secure web server where you can access the content. For example, your calendar wouldn't live on your Dell computer; it would live on Google's server, and you would access it with Google Calendar.

Drop-down menu: A menu type found in several Google tools. Drop-down menus provide users with additional options to help them find content. A drop-down menu is identified by an upside-down triangle.

Embed code: The Internet or HTML-based text can be copied from various web applications and pasted into a website or other tool.

Gadget: Small module of information on your iGoogle page. Gadgets are created by third-party developers and are available for you to add to your iGoogle page.

GB: Stands for gigabyte. It is a unit to measure the amount of space for computer storage; 1 GB equals 1,000 MB, or megabytes.

Hangout: A live video chat room in Google+ that can have 10 participants. You will need a webcam and microphone to make video chat work.

HTML: HyperText Markup Language. This is a programming code used to develop websites.

MB: Stands for megabyte. It is a unit to measure the amount of space for computer storage; 1 MB equals 1,000 KB, or kilobytes.

NETS: National Education Technology Standards. These standards are used to assess student, teacher, and administrator technology skills. The NETS are developed by ISTE (International Society for Technology Education).

Pixel: A pixel is a unit of measurement for determining the size of digital content. Your computer screen's resolution is measured in pixels.

Placemark: Icon indicating a location on a map. Placemarks are used in Google Earth, Picasa, and Google Maps.

PLN: Personal Learning Network. People use social media sites like Twitter, Facebook, Google+, and blogs to share information with colleagues as part of their PLN.

Real-time data: Indicates that the information provided on a website is updated within seconds to minutes. This information is dynamic and provides accurate content for the user.

RSS: Really Simple Syndication. RSS feeds are found on most blogs as a way to help users subscribe to content that is updated frequently. Google's Blogger has an RSS feed built into its service so you can share your blog with others.

Templates: Premade document files or website files you can use for your own classroom. You'll find templates in Google Sites and Google Docs.

URL: Universal Resource Locator. The URL is the online address for a particular website. It is located across the top of the Internet browser in the address bar.

Wiki: A webpage that allows collaboration among multiple people. Wikis are editable, and the changes are saved directly to the web. Wikis can be open to the public (e.g., Wikipedia), or they can be private, where a login/password is required to make changes.

References and Further Reading

21st Century Schools. (2010). *What is 21st century education?* Retrieved December 30, 2011, from http://www.21stcenturyschools.com/What_is_21st_Century_Education .htm

Anderson, N. (2006). *Teens: Email is for old people* [Web log message]. Retrieved December 30, 2011, from http://arstechnica.com/old/content/2006/10/7877.ars

Barnett, T. (2011). *The Google+ Project: Targeted sharing.* Retrieved January 4, 2012, from http://edte.ch/blog/2011/07/01/the-google-project-targeted-sharing/

Boss, S. (2008, November 13). *Teaching with visuals: Students respond to images.* Retrieved January 4, 2012, from http://www.edutopia.org/visuals-math-curriculum

Boss, S. (n.d.-a). *Google lit trips: Bringing travel tales to life.* Retrieved January 4, 2012, from http://www.edutopia.org/google-lit-trips-virtual-literature

Boss, S. (n.d.-b). *New York children take a Google Lit Trip.* Retrieved January 4, 2012, from http://www.edutopia.org/new-york

Bulley, B. (2011, January 23). *Heidi Rogers: Technology & community.* CDAPress.com. Retrieved January 4, 2012, from http://www.cdapress.com/lifestyles/article_2af7f86a-c3fb-5c7c-87c2-6e24d3ab7d0a.html

Carr, N. (2008, July). Is Google making us stupid? *The Atlantic.* Retrieved January 4, 2012, from http://www.theatlantic.com/magazine/archive/2008/07/is-google-making-us-stupid/6868/

Carvin, A. (2006, May 22). *What exactly is a blog, anyway?* Retrieved January 4, 2012, from http://www.pbs.org/teachers/learning.now/2006/05/what_exactly_is_a_blog_anyway.html

Cassinelli, C. (2008, November 4). *Tech Tip Tuesday—Google presentations* [Web log message]. Retrieved January 4, 2012, from http://edtechvision.org/?p=263

ConsumerSearch. (2011, July). *Google review.* Retrieved January 4, 2012, from http://www.consumersearch.com/search-engine-reviews/google

Curtis, E. (2011, June 28). *What does Google+ mean for schools?* Retrieved January 4, 2012, from http://www.appsusergroup.org/articles/what-does-googleplus-mean-for-schools

Dodge, B. (2007). *Webquest.org.* Retrieved January 4, 2012, from http://www.webquest.org/

Dretzin, R. (Executive Producer). (2010). Digital nation [Television series episode]. *Frontline.* Arlington, VA: Public Broadcasting Service.

Edutopia. (n.d.). *Multimedia serves youths' desire to express themselves.* Retrieved January 7, 2012, from http://www.edutopia.org/san-fernando-education-technology-multimedia.

Frontline. (2010, February 2). *Digital native map.* Retrieved January 4, 2012, from http://www.pbs.org/wgbh/pages/frontline/digitalnation/extras/digital_native.html . Arlington, VA: Public Broadcasting Service.

Gilbert, A. (2005, October 17). *Blogging 101—Web logs go to school.* Retrieved January 4, 2012, from http://news.cnet.com/Blogging-101--Web-logs-go-to-school/2100-1032_3-5895779.html

Google. (2011a). *Google for educators: Google Docs.* Retrieved January 4, 2012, from http://www.google.com/educators/p_docs.html

Google. (2011b). *Google for educators: The Google custom search engine.* Retrieved January 4, 2012, from http://www.google.com/educators/p_cse.html

Google. (2011d). *Ten reasons to choose Google Apps.* Retrieved January 4, 2012, from http://www.google.com/apps/intl/en/edu/sell.html

Google. (2011e). *Top ten advantages of Google's cloud.* Retrieved January 4, 2012, from http://www.google.com/apps/intl/en/business/cloud.html

Google. (2011f). *What are Google Alerts?* Retrieved January 4, 2012, from http://www.google.com/support/alerts/bin/static.py?page=guide.cs&guide=28413&topic=28416&answer=175927

Google. (n.d.-a). *Google in education.* Retrieved January 4, 2012, from http://www.google.com/edu/purpose.html

Google. (n.d.-b). *Inside search: Meet the new way to search: Google instant shows results as you type.* Retrieved January 4, 2012, from http://www.google.com/landing/instant/

Google. (n.d.). *Module 1: Google apps education edition.* Retrieved January 4, 2012, from http://edutraining.googleapps.com/Training-Home/module-1/chapter-1/3-1

Graves, M., Juel, C., & Graves, B. (2006). *Teaching reading in the 21st century* (4th ed.). Boston: Allyn & Bacon.

Hunt, J. (2010, February 8). *More creativity in the classroom* [Web log message]. Retrieved January 4, 2012, from http://www.huffingtonpost.com/jim-hunt/more-creativity-in-the-cl_b_453244.html

ISTE. (2007). *NETS for students 2007.* Retrieved January 4, 2012, from http://www.iste.org/standards/nets-for-students/nets-student-standards-2007.aspx

ISTE. (2008). *NETS for teachers 2008.* Retrieved January 4, 2012, from http://www.iste.org/standards/nets-for-teachers/nets-for-teachers-2008.aspx

Jackson, L. (2011, July 18). *Blogging? It's elementary, my dear Watson!* Retrieved January 4, 2012, from http://www.educationworld.com/a_tech/tech/tech217.shtml

Jackson, T. (2007, October 31). *How our spam filter works* [Web log message]. Retrieved January 4, 2012, from http://gmailblog.blogspot.com/2007/10/how-our-spam-filter-works.html

Jordan, J. (2008, October 28). *It's official—teens are getting dumber.* Retrieved January 7, 2012, from http://www.parentdish.com/2008/10/28/its-official-teens-getting-dumber/

McGee, M. (2010, February 23). *By the numbers: Twitter vs. Facebook vs. Google buzz.* Retrieved January 7, 2012, from http://searchengineland.com/by-the-numbers-twitter-vs-facebook-vs-google-buzz-36709

Melanson, M. (2010, July 30). *Google Earth shows real-time weather.* Retrieved January 7, 2012, from http://www.readwriteweb.com/archives/google_earth_shows_real-time_weather.php

Meloni, J. (2009, August 18). Getting started with Google Docs in the classroom. *Chronicle of Higher Education.* Retrieved January 7, 2012, from http://chronicle.com/blogPost/Getting-Started-with-Google/22641/

Nightingale, J. (2011, January 11). Get creative in school with digital media. *The Guardian.* Retrieved January 7, 2012, from http://www.guardian.co.uk/classroom-innovation/creative-schools-digital-media

Partnership for 21st Century Skills. (2004). Framework for 21st Century Learning. Retrieved January 7, 2012, from http://www.p21.org/overview/skills-framework

Paulson, F. L., Paulson, P. R., & Meyer, C. A. (1991). What makes a portfolio a portfolio? *Educational Leadership, 58*(5): 60–63.

Pearlman, B. (n.d.). *Students thrive on cooperation and problem solving.* Retrieved January 7, 2012, from http://www.edutopia.org/new-skills-new-century

Prensky, M. (2010) Digital nation [Television series episode]. In Dretzin, R. (Executive Producer), *Frontline*. New York: PBS.

Richardson, W. (2006, March 15). *The social web.* Retrieved January 7, 2012, from http://www.techlearning.com/article/the-social-web/43387

Rogers, M., Runyon, D., Starrett, D., & Von Holzen, R. (2006). *Teaching the 21st century learner.* Retrieved January 7, 2012, from https://docs.google.com/viewer?url=http://depd.wisc.edu/series/06_4168.pdf

Shelton, J. (2011, March 15). *Taking "boring" out of the classroom* [Web log message]. Retrieved January 7, 2012, from http://www.ed.gov/blog/2011/03/taking-"boring"-out-of-the-classroom/

Simple K12. (2010, November 11). *8 Google tricks for your classroom* [Web log message]. Retrieved January 7, 2012, from http://blog.simplek12.com/education/8-google-tricks-for-your-classroom/

Standen, A. (n.d.). *The good earth: See the world with Google's mapping program.* Retrieved January 7, 2012, from http://www.edutopia.org/google-earth-mapping-program-technology

Teacher Created Materials. (2002). *Why WebQuests.* Retrieved January 7, 2012, from http://www.internet4classrooms.com/why_webquest.htm

ThePicky. (2008). *Google handles 235 million searches per day.* Retrieved January 7, 2012, from http://www.thepicky.com/software/google-handles-235-million-searches-per-day/

Tumbleson, A. (2011, January 2). Students use Google Earth to explore the history of West. *West Yellowstone News.* Retrieved January 7, 2012, from http://www.westyellowstonenews.com/news/article_478521de-167c-11e0-afa2-001cc4c03286.html

Tyson, T. (2009). *Keynote address.* Presented at Utah Coalition for Education Technology conference, Salt Lake City. Retrieved January 5, 2012, from http://www.ucet.org/inUCETnew/archives/2009/conference/index.html

U.S. Department of Education. (2010). *National Education Technology Plan 2010.* Retrieved January 4, 2012, from http://www.ed.gov/technology/netp-2010

Watters, A. (2010, May 28). *The real time web & K–12 education—In and out of the classroom.* Retrieved January 7, 2012, from http://www.readwriteweb.com/archives/the_real_time_web_k-12_education_-_in_and_out_of_the_classroom.php

Index

Pages followed by f indicate figures.

CORWIN
A SAGE Company

The Corwin logo—a raven striding across an open book—represents the union of courage and learning. Corwin is committed to improving education for all learners by publishing books and other professional development resources for those serving the field of PreK–12 education. By providing practical, hands-on materials, Corwin continues to carry out the promise of its motto: **"Helping Educators Do Their Work Better."**